The Prophet Amos Speaks To America:

Ancient Wisdom For Contemporary Politics

Bruce G. Epperly

Energion Publications
Gonzalez, Florida
2022

ISBN: 978-1-63199-847-8
eISBN: 978-1-63199-848-5
Library of Congress Control Number: 2022947540

Energion Publications
P. O. Box 841
Gonzalez, FL 32560

energion.com
pubs@energion.com

TABLE OF CONTENTS

CHAPTER ONE

CONFESSIONS OF A GUILTY BYSTANDER

Take away from me the noise of your songs;
I will not listen to the melody of your harps.
But let justice roll down like waters,
and righteousness
like an ever-flowing stream.
(Amos 5:23-24)

We are all saints and prophets in the making! With no clear blueprint for our journey, we may discover that we are being touched by God's call to prayerful protest and to challenge the injustices of our time. We take our first steps toward the holy adventure of becoming prophets and saints when we hear the cries of vulnerable persons and experience the distance between God's vision and our own lifestyles and the values of our nation. In the words of Thomas Merton, we discover that although we aren't directly guilty for our nation's injustices, we are responsible for addressing the evils we observe. We can't unsee certain things and when we observe institutional injustice, violence, racism, or genocide, we are confronted with the choice – respond, deny, or withdraw. Touched by the pain of God's children, we can no longer accept injustice as normal and inevitable. We must, in a statement attributed to activist Angela Davis, "change what we cannot accept." That was Amos' challenge when God called him to journey from his privileged life as a sheepherder and orcharder to the Northern Kingdom of Israel to proclaim God's message of repentance and transformation.

On a lovely September morning, as a recently retired pastor, seeking to be a good ancestor by relocating to Bethesda, Maryland, to be closer to our elementary-age grandchildren, I found myself appalled by a headline that announced, "As billionaires grow richer, children wake up hungry." The author asserted that while the COVID pandemic has been an economic disaster for the poorest Americans, the global crisis has been a financial boon for America's wealthiest businesspeople and corporations. The author noted that, despite the benefits the most economically vulnerable Americans received from the COVID relief bill, the growing gap between the rich and poor is still widening.

The author correctly noted that this economic gap is not accidental but is the result of decades of tax policies that favor the wealthy at the expense of the most economically vulnerable Americans. In response to widening income inequality, the author suggested that "we must adjust the tax code that bends over backward for the extremely wealthy while treating those who struggle every day to afford food and housing as a burden."[1]

A few weeks later, I read another analysis describing the economic gains by billionaires during the pandemic. The article noted that American billionaires' wealth increased by 62% during the pandemic, raising their assets to nearly five trillion.[2] America is not alone in promoting the interests of the wealthy over the poor and shrinking middle class. On the global stage, it has been reported that "the world's 2,365 billionaires enjoyed a $4 trillion boost to their wealth during the first year of the pandemic, increasing their fortunes by 54%, according to a new analysis by the Program on Inequality of the Institute for Policy Studies." As one commentator noted, "our pain is their gain."[3]

Poverty is epidemic in the United States. While the US Census Bureau estimated that 34 million or 10.5% of Americans can be described as poor, Inequality.org, a project of the Institute of Policy Studies, counters that the official poverty rate understates

1   Diane Randall, "As billionaires grow richer, children go hungry. Religion News Service, September 27, 2021.

2   Chuck Collins, "U.S. Billionaires Got 62 percent Richer During Pandemic. They're Now Up $1.8 Trillion," Institute for Policy Studies, August 24, 2021.

3   Aimee Pichie, "Billionaires Get 54% Richer During Pandemic, Sparking Calls for 'Wealth Tax,'" CBS News Money Watch, March 31, 2021.

the number of people who have trouble making ends meet, families who live month to month and for whom an unplanned car repair or visit to the emergency room can be a financial catastrophe. According to Poverty.org, an estimated 40 percent of the total U.S. population (140 million people) are either poor or low-income.[4] Both estimates of American poverty are appalling, given the growing wealth gap and the astounding financial gains of the top 1/10 of 1% of Americans.

In terms of national policy, America clearly privileges the wealthy over the working or unemployed poor. Despite the disparity of wealth and poverty, many Americans, even those of the lower middle class, believe that the wealthy deserve their wealth and will always use it wisely and for the greater good while the poor are responsible for their poverty, will waste any government subsidies, and must justify the slightest extravagance. Yet, if we open the doors of perception, we will see the truth clearly: it's hard work to be poor and traumatizing to parents and children to be part of the welfare system, living on the edge of destitution, and forced to justify every expenditure or source of income. Moreover, it's expensive to be poor. Not having a car reduces a person's ability to shop for bargains at grocery and retail stores. Further, if you lack a car, you must spend more of your discretionary time on public transportation, which is woefully inadequate in many parts of the United States. If we open our minds and hearts to the realities of wealth and poverty, we will discover that if the wealthiest Americans would make modest – and dare we say, unnoticeable - sacrifices through the interplay of greater generosity, more equitable wages and benefits, and higher tax rates to promote the greater good, and in recognition of the advantages they receive in terms of governmental subsidized infrastructure and services, the most vulnerable Americans, including those described by the term "working poor," would have a fair chance to improve their lives and their children's futures.

---

4   Income Inequality - Inequality.org

I must confess that I did not intend to write this book. In fact, it is a very difficult subject for me, as an affluent American, blessed by generous pension plans, and trying to live by biblical values, to address. Amos agitates our spirits and provides, at first glance, very little comfort to the "haves" of this world, including middle/upper-middle-class people like myself. The prophet denounces any system, whether in 8th century BCE Israel or 21st century America that promotes significant income disparity and puts profit ahead of the needs of the poor. Still, despite my initial uneasiness at embarking on this project, I intuitively knew I had to study what the prophet Amos would have to say to twenty-first-century America. I had to consider what his challenge, indeed, Amos' spiritual mantra, "Let justice roll down like water, and righteousness like an ever-flowing stream," would mean to me and to other privileged Americans. (Amos 5:24) In focusing on Amos' words to the United States, I am not excluding people of other nations. I believe that Amos' words are global, and not bound by time and place. He is speaking to the leaders of the Northern Kingdom of Israel some 2700 years ago, but sensitive spirits have heard his words echoing in their own political and economic context throughout the ages, whether their home was Washington D.C.; London, England; Glasgow, Scotland; Vancouver, British Columbia; or Bogota, Columbia. Ancient, they are also present and future; localized, they are also global; contextual, they are also universal.

As an author of books in theology, spirituality, and healing, I have come to believe that my writing is often the result of a gentle and sometimes disturbing providence that moves through my life providing synchronous encounters, disturbing newsfeeds, and moments of unanticipated inspiration, pushing me to address subjects I might otherwise avoid. This book emerged when I heard a voice, not a shout from heaven or a command from a demanding deity, but a still small voice, an inner inclination not entirely my own, during my morning walk through my upscale suburban Washington DC neighborhood. Welling up from within my predawn ruminations, a voice whispered, "You need to write something about what the prophet Amos would say to today's America and to people like you. You need to listen to Amos as if he is speaking upper middle class and middle class people like you and to our political and business leaders and those who benefit from their decisions. You need to ask: How can Amos shape your own politics and economic decision-making to be aligned with God's vision? You need to ask: How can your love for your grandchildren challenge you to care for other people's children, children you will never meet, and future generations of children who will be born long after you're gone?"

Although I am a student of mysticism and take spiritual practices seriously, I am prone to understate my own experiences of the Holy and never blithely assume that God is the source of my insights. My fallibility and self-interest are obvious to me. I have seen too many religious prevaricators and manipulators who claim to be speaking for God but are only fleecing the public, selling fake news, or raising persons' hopes that Jesus will return to solve all their problems and destroy their enemies while we wait passively on the sidelines.

Yet, despite my agnosticism about most "God said to me" acclamations, I believe that God is inspiring each of us moment by moment and encounter by encounter. I believe each moment has a vocation that emerges through the interplay of environment, previous history, personal choice, and divine presence. God gives each of us messages appropriate to our time and place. I believe that God may even be speaking to me – and to you – calling us from quietism to prophetic healing and privilege to activism.

My understanding of divine inspiration prompted me to take my early morning guidance seriously just as Amos took seriously the word of God that came to him, perhaps in a moment of leisure, while reveling in the beauty of a sunrise, or supervising his shepherds. (Amos 1:1, 7:15) I asked for wisdom. I listened prayerfully. Although the inner voice gave me but scant direct guidance, nothing more than the push in the direction of writing a text, I trusted its message and knew I had to follow. I had to trust the voice not only for my own spiritual edification but as a message to privileged persons like myself. I needed to find a way to share a prophetic word not in terms of a presumptuous "thus saith the Lord" demanding obedience to my words but as a humble companion and "guilty bystander," to use the phrase of Trappist mystic Thomas Merton, to my fellow Americans who are also, like me, struggling to follow their conscience, and awaken to divine guidance, in their lives as citizens of the most powerful and prosperous nation on the planet. I needed to think and write and eventually find ways to act to fulfill my vocation as God's companion in healing the spirit of America and ultimately the planet.

Amos presents a difficult message to persons like us, living comfortably and certain of our next meal, and having the leisure and education for reading and study. Amos takes no prisoners in his challenging, if not damning message, to our nation's political and economic leaders, who refuse to respond to the handwriting on the wall, etched by forest fires and floods, foreclosures and evictions, hopelessness in inner cities and rural Appalachia, the opioid crisis and profiteering of pharmaceutical companies, refugees on our borderlands, attacks on democracy and racist rhetoric from elected leaders, policing that terrorizes persons of color, and growing anger at scientists and physicians for suggesting people limit their personal freedoms to respond compassionately to the COVID pandemic. Power and prevarication, and division and destruction, characterize much of our politics. Although his voice was more strident, the prophet Amos stands with another prophet, the Athenian philosopher Socrates, in his condemnation of the most educated and affluent of the Greek city-states, fourth-century B.C.E. Athens. In words that could easily be addressed to America's intellectual and economic elite, Socrates chides:

> You are an Athenian, a citizen of the greatest city with the greatest reputation for both wisdom and power; are you not ashamed of your eagerness to possess as much wealth, reputation and honors as possible, while you do not care for nor

give thought to wisdom and truth, or the best possible state of your soul? (Apology 29d)

We need only substitute Washington, DC or Montgomery, Alabama, or Mar-a-Lago or Silicon Valley, for Bethel or Samaria, to feel the spirit of Amos' critique of our nation when we fail to respond to the cries of the poor or the stranger at the gate. Marianne Williamson, Jon Meacham, and Joe Biden speak of healing the soul of America and Amos would concur that the spirit of our nation, like the Northern Kingdom of Israel, needs healing and that the healing we need often comes with a cost. We require spiritual surgery and a radically transformed political and economic system to find national healing. There is no cheap grace or painless institutional healing for Amos. Sacrifices must be made by those who can afford to sacrifice and whose affluence is in stark contrast with the poverty of their neighbors. If we fail to hear the cries of the poor – if we are complicit in injustice – our nation will not only collapse; we will soon be unable to hear God's voice. As the prophet says, there will be a famine of hearing God's word. (Amos 8:11-12)

As Amos contends, God hears the cries of the poor, and God's voice speaking through their pain challenges all of us, but most especially those wielding power and enjoying prosperity, to listen to God's messages spoken through the voices of the voiceless, homeless, evicted, malnourished, desperate, and hopeless, whether in Appalachian coal country, inner-city Chicago, or a campsite for unhoused people in Los Angeles. Hearing their voices requires a response, and responding necessitates political, economic, and personal sacrifice, and the willingness to let go of power and privilege so that others can simply survive.

Hearing God's voice, truly hearing God's message, demands transformation. We receive new possibilities and responsibilities, sometimes a new name, and always a transformed lifestyle if we are to be faithful to God's calling. For privileged persons like myself – and most of my readers – this means advocacy for social transformation, justice, and earth care, and sacrifice of comfort and largesse for the greater good of the voiceless, "the least of these," in our midst. I believe that this is the call of Amos to America today.

This text reflects my personal dialogue and struggle with the message of the prophet Amos, shaped by my desire to be faithful to God's vision of Shalom as I live out my vocation as a citizen, consumer, pastor, professor, husband, and grandparent. I am a contemplative and academic, not a political activist, by disposition. Like Amos, I am not by vocation a prophet or activist, and unsure if I will ever claim those titles. I am not a William Barber, Greta Thunberg, Dorothy Day, Martin Luther King, Oscar Romero, Fannie Lou Hamer, Jeremiah Wright, or John Lewis. And yet God calls me, as God called them, through the cries of the poor, the despair of the marginalized, and the reality of environmental devastation to do what I can to be God's companion in healing the world.

I don't think Amos sought to uproot himself from the comforts of home to travel to the Northern Kingdom prior to his unsettling encounter with the Holy One. And yet God speaks to us and through us, as God did to the prosperous herdsman and farmer Amos, inviting us to listen and respond. Like Amos, we must pray, and we must also protest, using our unique gifts to tip the balance from death to life. "Weak resignation to the evils we deplore," as Harry Emerson Fosdick writes, is not an option if we are to be faithful to God's vision.

The flow of this text will involve an interplay of yesterday, today, and tomorrow. We will reflect on Amos' message, first delivered to the Northern Kingdom of Israel over 2,800 years ago. We will explore the meaning of the Book of Amos for ourselves and 21st-century economics, politics, and foreign policy, and reflect on the impact of our responses on the future, our own and that of generations to come, as well as the impact of our choices for our nation and the planet. Amos' challenge is not just to the United States but is addressed to the economically and politically powerful, the elite, of every nation. However, as an American, I believe that if the scriptures have any relevance at all, and are not merely an historical era piece, we must hear them addressed to us in the concreteness of our personal and political lives, especially those of us who live in a democracy, believe we can make a difference, and enjoy the benefits of living in the most affluent and powerful nation in the world. We must ask, "What would Amos say to Americans in the 2020s? What would Amos say to our leaders and to the leaders of nations with whom we compete militarily and economically?"

Clearly, our economic and governmental system is very different from that of the Northern Kingdom, Israel, in the 8th century before the birth of Jesus. Moreover, there is no one-to-one correspondence between the issues Amos addresses and the religious, political, and economic challenges of our technologically advanced and religiously pluralistic time. Amos' prophetic words need to be adapted to our time and place. If the scriptures are to be relevant to persons and institutions, we must affirm an ongoing dialogue between the biblical witness and our current situation. Inspiration is always concrete and timely, whether found in the words of Amos speaking to the temple priest of Bethel or William Barber leading the Poor Peoples' Campaign or Greta Thunberg challenging the world leaders to respond quickly to the dangers of climate change, or Pastor Jeremiah Wright damning America for the economics and politics of racism. God is still speaking, and the prophetic voices speak anew to every generation.

I must confess that although I have written several books on biblical texts, I am not by training a biblical scholar just Amos claimed, in response to the Temple priest Amaziah's critique, not to be a professional prophet. (Amos 7:10-14) Perhaps, theological and ethical reflection, and the interplay of action and reflection in the realm of economics and politics, are too important to be left solely to scholars. I am a pastor, theologian, spiritual teacher, and American citizen, for whom the Bible provides insights into how we should respond to issues of ethics, ecology, race, and politics. I deal with the interplay of the personal and planetary, and concrete human and non-human experience to bring life to abstract theological concepts. Accordingly, this text is intended to be a theological and spiritual reflection, an imaginative epistle addressed

to twenty-first-century Americans. While grounded in solid biblical scholarship, this text aims at whole person transformation and
seeks to explore Amos as a living companion, one who loved his
people but was also, as a member of my seminar on Amos asserted,
"a pain in the ass."

Amos is speaking to us boldly and directly. We may challenge
Amos' view of divine intervention in history and understanding of
divine punishment – and I will offer alternative visions of divine
power and presence – but still, the words of Amos ring true, if only
we listen and then change our ways.

I am grateful to the members of the "Prophet Amos Speaks
to America" seminar, sponsored on Zoom by Westmoreland Congregational United Church of Christ, Bethesda, Maryland, and
reaching out to persons across the United States. I am grateful
to pastors Tim Tutt and Kaeley McEvoy who invited me to lead
this study. My reflections have benefited from the input of the
seminar members. Although this text began with a moment of
quiet inspiration on a Bethesda, Maryland street, I believe that
revelation always requires a receiver or a group of receivers, who
shape and interpret their experiences of the Holy, thus giving flesh
to the bones of my lectures. Still, I take responsibility for this text
– as Amos likely took responsibility for his words to the Northern
Kingdom – joining my own fallibility with God's call to move from
self-interest and privilege, and, in my case, intellectual, economic,
and spiritual privilege, to world loyalty. With Reinhold Niebuhr,
I believe that I must recognize truth in what I perceive to be my
neighbor's falsehood and the falsehood – the limitations – of my
most cherished truths, even as I affirm the importance of the words
I share.

To be true to Amos' message, our contemplation must lead
to action and advocacy, appropriate to our gifts, social position,
and context. It is my hope that I – along with those who read this
text – will be challenged to explore the meaning of God's vision of
Shalom and to claim our vocation as God's companions in healing

the earth, so that "justice [will] roll down like waters, and righteousness like an ever-flowing stream." (Amos 5:24)

This is an "American" text. I have used the words "United States of America" and "American" as synonyms throughout this text. I am not privileging the status of "USAmericans" and recognize that we are not the only Americans. Still, the word "America" is in our nation's name and most of our American partners choose to use more specific names, "Canadian," "Mexican," "Costa Rican," and "Brazilian," for example, to describe their citizenship. While it may be a form of exceptionalism, most USA citizens of all ethnicities use "American" to describe themselves, even when they criticize the USA. I am writing to USAmericans calling them to economic and political transformation, grounded in spiritual transformation, so that we can become "exceptional" as lights for justice and peace in the years to come.

In conclusion, I dedicate this book, first, to my grandchildren and their peers, that they may grow up in a just and eco-friendly world in which all the colors of the rainbow are treasured and affirmed. I also dedicate this book to Rev. Michael-Ray Mathews, my father's pastor, prophetic pathfinder, preacher, and friend.

LISTENING TO THE VOICE OF THE PROPHET AMOS

Each chapter will conclude with questions for reflection, aimed at making the text come alive in our concrete situation as 21st century Americans as well as a spiritual practice, intended to awaken to God's voice in our personal lives and political involvement. Theological and biblical reflection finds its completion in contemplative activism, the holistic integration of mind, body, spirit, and action.

Spiritual Practice. We begin this study with a time of stillness, breathing deeply the Spirit of Truth, letting it fill your mind, body, and spirit, and exhaling with a sense of the impact of your life on the world around you. Feel your connectedness with God and all creation, most especially those who struggle for survival in the United States and around the globe.

In the stillness, and throughout the days ahead, ask God, or whatever you deem the source of revelation and moral guidance, to give you insights into the challenges our nation faces, your unintended complicity in injustice, and your role in responding to these challenges. Perhaps you might pray some version of the following: "Where do I need to awaken to the cries of the vulnerable? How can I be of service to the vulnerable and forgotten? How can I best advocate for the least of these?" Ask God to help you experience the world in its tragic beauty from God's perspective, feeling God's empathy with suffering. Ask God to show you the way forward from self-interest to sacrificial living for the forgotten and marginalized.

QUESTIONS FOR REFLECTION

1) When you hear the words, "let justice roll down like waters, and righteousness like an ever-flowing stream," what images come to mind? How might these words concretely relate to the United States – its hopes, history, and current challenges?

2) Have you ever experienced the "still, small voice" of inspiration? Did you connect it with God? What was its content? What was your response to this "mystical" moment?

3) What is the nature of our input in response to divine inspiration? Do we shape – and how shall we shape – the messages we may attribute to divine providence?

4) What does it mean to be a "guilty bystander?" In what ways might you be described as a "guilty bystander?" In what ways does recognizing the accuracy of this description require you to change spiritually, ethically, or politically?

5) How would you describe the political, economic, and judicial condition of the United States today?

6) How do respond to the statement made earlier in the text: "we must adjust the tax code that bends over backward for the extremely wealthy while treating those who struggle every day to afford food and housing as a burden.?" How are the wealthy and poor, respectively viewed by citizens and politicians in the United States? Is this perception accurate? What prejudices do you have about the poor and those receiving government aid?

Prayer. Challenge, God of All Peoples, my complacency. Open my senses to the cries of the poor. Awaken me to my complicity in the pain of others. Give me courage to move from apathy to empathy and passivity to agency in responding to the needs of others, personally and politically. Help me to be your companion in letting "justice roll down like waters, and righteousness like an ever-flowing stream." Amen.

CHAPTER TWO

THE PROPHETIC VISION

In the year King Uzziah died,
I saw the Lord sitting on a throne...
I heard the voice of God saying,
"Whom shall I send and who will go for us?"
And I said, "Here I am, send me."
(Isaiah 6:1, 8)

The United Church of Christ has as one of its affirmations, "God is still speaking." This bold declaration has often provoked the response, "Is anyone listening?" Prophets are persons who listen. They listen to God and attend to the signs of the times. A North African desert father once spoke of the monk as "all eye." Prophets are not only all eye, but all ear, nose, touch, throat, and taste. Tuned into the signs of times at the marketplace and in the media, they are also all heart and mind, dedicated to God and God's vision of Shalom and attentive to the pain of the vulnerable and forgotten.

Prophets are mystics and spirit persons, to use the description of biblical theologian Marcus Borg. They experience the Holy as a palpable reality and then share their experiences of divine communication with their contemporaries. Prophets listen deeply. They hear God's whispers in the cries of the poor. The feel God's heartbeat in the anxiety of the homeless and vulnerable. They intuit emptiness and despair behind wealthy walled communities and in the hearts of celebrity politicians. What they experience is never spirituality in general, and never abstract and irrelevant to the human condition, but concrete spirituality mediated through God's presence moving in the spiritual and moral arcs of history.

I believe that deep down, we are all mystics. God touches all of us. But few of us allow God's presence to define our experience of the world and determine our daily lives. Like Amos, few mystics set out to become agents of God's vision. They are people just like us, making a living, caring for families, and trying to be good citizens, to whom God speaks. Even more remarkably, they listen and then respond, despite the potential threats to reputation and personal safety.

The age of prophetic and mystical experience continues in our time, and in the encounter with God, we receive a vocation and then the courage and energy to share God's vision with others. There is a prophet and mystic in each of us, showing itself whenever we feel distress at the pain of others and want to right the wrongs around us. There is a prophet ready to come out as we feel our hearts beating in synch with the oppressed and forgotten.

Listen to Martin Luther King's description of a mystical experience that transformed his life and gave him courage to continue his prophetic ministry. One evening, the young preacher King received an angry phone call, threatening his life and the lives of his wife and children. Unable to sleep, King went downstairs to brew a pot of coffee. In his moment of crisis, King felt a Presence that gave him strength for the journey.

> I was ready to give up. I tried to think of a way to move out of the picture without appearing to be a coward. In this state of exhaustion, when my courage was almost gone, I determined to take my problem to God. My head in my hands, I bowed over the kitchen table and prayed aloud.... "I am here taking a stand for what I believe is right. But now I am afraid. The people are looking to me for leadership, and if I stand before them without strength or courage, they too will falter. I am at the end of my powers. I have nothing left. I've come to the point where I can't face it alone."

In the midnight hour, King encounters the Living God, whose love envelopes us in life and death.

> At that moment I experienced the presence of the divine as I had never experienced him. It seems as though I could hear the quiet assurance of an inner voice, saying, "Stand up

for righteousness, stand up for truth, God will be at your side forever.[5]

King continues, "the outer situation remained the same, but God had given me inner calm."[6] Three days later, King's home was bombed. But King remained rooted in God's faithfulness, knowing that nothing can separate us from the love of God.

Trappist monk Thomas Merton, who retreated from the academic world to find God in monastic living, encountered God in the hustle and bustle of Louisville, Kentucky.

> At the corner of Fourth and Walnut, in the center of the shopping district, I was suddenly overwhelmed with the realization that I loved all those people, that they were mine and I was theirs, that we could not be alien to one another even though we were total strangers.
>
> It was like waking from a dream of separateness…The whole illusion of separate holy existence is a dream.[7]

In that moment, Merton realized that there is no "other." Saint and sinner, monk and politician, enlightened and benighted, and sacred and secular, are joined in divine unity. Our only response to experiencing mystic unity is gratitude and empathy, feeling the heartbeat of creation beating in our own hearts. Despite his commitment to monastic solitude, Merton affirmed, "Thank God, thank God that I *am* like other men, that I am only a man among others."[8] We are all one in the Spirit and one in God's love.[9]

---

5   Martin Luther King, Jr. *Testament of Hope: The Essential Writings and Speeches of Martin Luther King, Jr.* (edited by James M. Washington), (New York: HarperSanFrancisco, 1986), 509.

6   Martin Luther King, Jr. *Testament of Hope: The Essential Writings and Speeches of Martin Luther King, Jr.* (edited by James M. Washington), (New York: HarperSanFrancisco, 1986), 509.

7   Thomas Merton, *Essential Writings,* edited by Christine M. Bochen (Maryknoll, NY: Orbis Books, 2000) 90.

8   Ibid., 91.

9   For more on contemplative spirituality, see Bruce Epperly, *Mystics in Action: Twelve Saints for Today* (Maryknoll, NY: Orbis Press, 2020.

The Mechanics of Prophetic Spirituality. In her sensitive portrayal of a Syrian refugee couple, *The Beekeeper of Aleppo,* author Christy Lefteri confesses that her writing was driven by the question, "What does it mean to see?" Prophets are people who see. They also feel. What is repressed, hidden, or simply overlooked by others resounds in prophetic spirituality. There is no denial of the pain of the world and the reality that much of this pain is the result of human choices, including those of the privileged and powerful. The prophets see the hidden realities of life and although they don't predict the future in its details or have a timeline for healing or destruction, they see where the road of injustice and idolatry is leading for individuals and nations. To the prophet, the world is beautiful and God-filled, and it is also tragic.

While prophets are inspired by a divine call that transforms their lives and gives them a vocation to be God's emissaries to wayward communities, prophetic experience varies from person to person. Mystics and prophets are not passive recipients of revelation. Revelation requires a receiver, whose experience is shaped by their historical context, religious symbols, life history, and personality. Prophets are not drones or robots, but unique flesh and blood respondents to divine revelation. Prophetic mysticism widens and enhances creativity and freedom rather than diminishes them. The prophetic conscience may, as in the case of Amos, cause the prophet to challenge God's intentions, and God's threat to destroy the Northern Kingdom. A prophet may even reluctantly join God's cause as did Jonah, who despite his experiences of divine mercy, remained ambivalent about God's willingness to save his nation's arch enemy, the city of Nineveh. As artists of spiritual and political transformation, prophets contribute their own palette to the canvas of revelation. While true to God's vision and vocation for them, they have the freedom to express God's call in their own unique ways. Inspired and shaped by their encounter with God, it is still the prophet's voice that their community hears. Their "thus saith the Lord" reveals God's intentions in the unique interactions of prophetic speech, conveyed though their own experiences and the community's response to the prophet's words of protest and challenge.

The Prophetic Encounter. While God is always moving through our lives and history, there are moments in which the creative word of God comes alive for us. The complications of life remain, and we must continue to deal with our own imperfections and the complexities of personal relationships and citizenship, but now we experience these from a wider perspective, the Divine Vision or, as Abraham Joshua Heschel, avers, the Divine Pathos, God's empathy with humankind in its suffering. Steeped in their own culture, history, ethnicity, and unique personality, prophets experience God's vision as shaping the entirety of their experience and giving them clear direction in life. The prophet becomes a new creation, mediating God's challenging word to changing historical situations.

Scripture describes the prophetic encounter in a variety of ways, sometimes dramatic, other times, understated, but always life transforming. Amos' describes his mystical encounter with God in the simplest of ways.

> The Lord said to me, "Go, prophesy to my people Israel."
> (Amos 7:15)

As the prophetic text begins, the Book of Amos describes his experience in autobiographical terms without flourish:

> The words of Amos…which he saw concerning Israel in
> the days of King Uzziah of Judah and in the days of Jeroboam
> son of Joash of Israel, two years before the earthquake.
> (Amos 1:1-2)

Yet Amos' descriptive simplicity points to his profound encounter with the Holy One, which includes a demand, message, inspiration, and historical context. God is embedded in history, the most moved mover, infinitely intimate, embracing all creation and yet noting the fall of a sparrow and a hungry child's plea. Revelation comes to a particular person at a particular time to a particular people. The Infinite meets the finite, the Everlasting meets the everchanging, the Eternal meets the fleeting, and it is holy ground, revealing a holy mission.

Let's take a moment to look at another prophetic encounter. Perhaps, two decades after Amos, Isaiah's prophetic call is dramatic and turns the prophet's world upside down. Still, like Amos, Isaiah's encounter with the Holy One is rooted in history and comes with a task, speaking God's message to a wayward people. God's call is always personal and yet global, taking the prophet from self-preoccupation to world loyalty.

> In the year that King Uzziah died, I saw the Lord sitting on a throne, high and lofty; and the hem of his robe filled the temple. Seraphs were in attendance above him; each had six wings: with two they covered their faces, and with two they covered their feet, and with two they flew. And one called to another and said:
>
> "Holy, holy, holy is the Lord of hosts; the whole earth is full of his glory."
>
> The pivots on the thresholds shook at the voices of those who called, and the house filled with smoke. And I said: "Woe is me! I am lost, for I am a man of unclean lips, and I live among a people of unclean lips; yet my eyes have seen the King, the Lord of hosts!"
>
> Then one of the seraphs flew to me, holding a live coal that had been taken from the altar with a pair of tongs. The seraphs touched my mouth with it and said: "Now that this has touched your lips, your guilt has departed and your sin is blotted out." Then I heard the voice of the Lord saying, "Whom shall I send, and who will go for us?" And I said, "Here am I; send me!" (Isaiah 6:1-8)

Isaiah's experience is overwhelming and unexpected. We don't know about his previous experiences of God. Isaiah was, no doubt, a regular temple goer but none of his previous experiences prepared him for encountering the god of the universe. Obviously literate and intellectual, and no doubt among the elite of the nation, Isaiah experiences his insignificance and imperfection in relationship to the God of the Universe. Still, God works through his gifts and his access to the religious and political leadership of the Southern Kingdom. As some scholars suggest, Isaiah may have been aware of Amos' prophetic ministry, given the similarity of some passages in Amos to the message of Isaiah and his followers.[10]

God calls to another prophet, the youthful Jeremiah, reminding him that despite his age, he will be God's voice of challenge and repentance, warning the people of the consequences of turning from God to idols of their own making. Like Amos, Jeremiah's encounter with the Living God involves both words and images, and similar in address to Isaiah's temple encounter, Jeremiah's mystical experience involves God's touch as well:

> Now the word of the LORD came to me saying,
> "Before I formed you in the womb I knew you, and before you were born I consecrated you; I appointed you a prophet to the nations."
> Then I said, "Ah, Lord GOD! Truly I do not know how to speak, for I am only a boy." But the LORD said to me, "Do not say, 'I am only a boy'; for you shall go to all to whom I send you, and you shall speak whatever I command you. Do not be afraid of them, for I am with you to deliver you, says the LORD."
> Then the LORD put out his hand and touched my mouth; and the LORD said to me, "Now I have put my words in your mouth. See, today I appoint you over nations and over kingdoms, to pluck up and to pull down, to destroy and to overthrow, to build and to plant."
> The word of the LORD came to me, saying, "Jeremiah, what do you see?" And I said, "I see a branch of an almond tree." (Jeremiah 1:4-11)

None of these prophets sought their appointment. Still, there was something in their character that was transparent to God's call. Had God previously called to others who declined the divine mission? Regardless of God's address to others, the Hebraic proph-

---

10 Scholars believe that Isaiah may have been compiled by at least three "authors" given the text's varied theological and historical emphases.

ets said "yes" to the divine summons, following God's vision and vocation despite all their fear and trembling.

Heschel, Brueggemann, and Thurman on the Mysticism and Politics of Prophetic Experience. Some of the most perceptive descriptions of prophetic experience have come from Rabbi Abraham Joshua Heschel, United Church of Christ pastor and biblical scholar Walter Brueggemann, and African American mystic Howard Thurman. Their work reveals the interplay of empathy, imagination, and protest in prophetic ministry. They present a vision of prophetic mystics who are both heavenly minded and earthly good.

Perhaps the most important book on the prophets is Abraham Joshua Heschel's two-volume text, *The Prophets.* At the heart of Heschel's interpretation of the Hebraic prophets is his concept of Divine Pathos, in which God "does not reveal himself in absolute abstractness, but in personal and intimate relationship to the world. He does not simply command and expect obedience; He is also moved and affected by what happens in the world an reacts accordingly. Events and human actions arouse in Him joy or sorrow, pleasure or wrath."[11] Pathos is the commitment of the Infinite to the finite, the Eternal to the temporal, God to humankind. God hears the cries of the poor and feels the pain of the world. God has a stake in the world and needs humankind to achieve God's purposes. We are God's companions in healing the planet or opponents destroying the earth, and this is done one moment, one decision, one public policy, and one boardroom priority at a time. As Heschel claims, "the rabbis were not guilty of exaggeration in asserting, 'Whoever destroys a single soul should be considered the same as one who destroyed a whole world. And whoever saves one single soul should be considered the same as one who has saved a whole world.'"[12] While maintaining their personal identity, the prophets see the world from the point of view of God. They also feel the divine empathy, God's pain at illness,

---

11   Abraham Joshua Heschel, *The Prophets* (Peabody, MA: Hendrickson, 1962), volume 2, 3-4.
12   Ibid., volume 1, 14.

injustice, and violence, much of which is the result of personal and institutional decision-making. Just as God constantly influences our lives, whatever we do also affects God's experience. "Pathos means: God is never neutral, never beyond good and evil. He is always partial to justice."[13]

Prophets do not, according to Heschel predict the future in terms of the details of what is to come. Their messages are more like that of the Ghost of Christmas Future from Charles Dickens' *Christmas Carol*, describing what will happen – Tiny Tim's death and his own lonely death and burial – unless Ebenezer Scrooge mends his ways. The same applies to the affairs of institutions and nations. The prophets believe that the future is open for God and us. When we change our ways, we may avoid catastrophe. But, if we fail to hear God's warnings, catastrophe is likely to occur, either through nature, internal strife, or external threat.

Prophets believe that our committed acts of justice-seeking and compassion enable God to be more active in the world to champion for justice and planetary wellbeing. While God's existence does not depend on us, God needs us to be God's hands, heart, and feet in the world. Accordingly, the prophet calls us to listen to "the voice that God has lent to the silent agony, a voice to the plundered poor, to the profaned riches of the world."[14]

With all their personal limitations and fallibilities, and anger and frustration, prophets seek to portray the divine passion for justice. Though contemplative in spirit, the prophets also reflect the divine restlessness embodied in the moral and spiritual arcs of history. Contemporary prophetic voices like Martin Luther King, who challenged the ubiquity of American racism and its deadening impact on African Americans, and John Cobb, who penned the first theological text on ecology, describe the divine impulse toward planetary and institutional healing respectively with provocative comments, "Why we can't wait" and "Is it too late?" God's love is universal, embracing rich and poor, and oppressor and oppressed,

---

13 Ibidl, vol. 2, 11.
14 Ibid., vol 1, 5.

and yet God has a "preferential option" for the poor, whose cries break God's heart. God also experiences the moral bankruptcy of political demagogues whose pretense hides their spiritual emptiness and whose spiritual emptiness must be filled by power and possession.

According to theologian and Hebraic scripture scholar Walter Brueggemann, prophetic ministry involves "direct, confrontational encounter with established power," whether religious, economic, or political.[15] Words matter, and prophets are wordsmiths, whose prophetic speech enables us to envision alternative worlds and open to both the hope and threat of imaginative futures. "The task of prophetic ministry [whether in Israel or the United States] is to nurture, nourish, and evoke a consciousness and perception alternative to the consciousness and perception of the dominant culture around us."[16] The prophet proclaims a spiritual alternative to the "religion of static triumphalism and the politics of oppression and exploitation."[17]

God cannot be domesticated. Nor can God be the justification of our nation's – or Judah's or Israel's – economic, political, and religious practices. As C.S. Lewis describes Aslan in *The Lion, The Witch, and the Wardrobe,* the Holy One is good but not safe! At the heart of the prophetic message is the challenge to go beyond complacency and exceptionalism to lament. "Real criticism begins in the capacity to grieve because that is the most visceral announcement that things are not right."[18] Amos prods the wealthy and powerful to recognize the connection between their largesse and others' poverty, and to awaken them to the cries of the poor. Our hearts must be pierced. Denial, numbness, and apathy must give way to regret, confession, and repentance. The lamentations of the wealthy must join the daily lament of the poor and vulnerable. The

---

15   Walter Brueggemann, *The Prophetic Imagination* (Minneapolis: Fortress Press, 2001), ix.

16   Ibid., 3.

17   Ibid., 5.

18   Ibid., 11.

capacity to grieve will save us from the consequences of our denial and the consequent famine of hearing God's word. Confession and lamentation are the foundation of national healing, the inspiration to personal and political transformation.

Prophets imagine alternative realities and ask, "Why not? Why can't we embody the promise of liberty and justice for all?" Prophets put themselves in the place of the impoverished and forgotten, the grieving and traumatized. They invite us to visualize our common humanity and see ourselves in the frantic Haitian, Afghan, Guatemalan, and Ukrainian immigrant, the Appalachian parent feeling that life has passed by themselves and their family, the inner city child whose sleep is interrupted by gunshots, the First American parent struggling to make ends meet and achieve a better future for their children, the angry white nationalist who projects his hate on immigrants and marginalized persons like themselves rather than the economic and political systems that cause their poverty and powerlessness.

Prophets imaginatively see the world as it could be if the powerful and privileged sacrificed for the greater good – laughter in the city streets, blue skies and clean water, celebration on tribal lands, children achieving their full potential, and families delighting in safe and comfortable shelter, education, and nutrition. All this is possible, the prophet believes, but it requires a great imaginative leap – the willingness of the powerful and privileged to lament and sacrifice – as we move from self-interest to human-heartedness and earth care. The powerful and privileged must, to use the language of Joanna Rogers Macy, do their own "despair work," facing their fear of change, their captivity to the status quo and its destructive power, and the necessity of sacrifice for planetary survival. We must minimally live more simply and advocate for social, political, and economic transformation so others may simply live. While the prophets recognize the need for the powerless and vulnerable to advocate for justice, living between lamentation and hope, their denunciations are aimed at the powerful whose transformation is necessary for God's Shalom to take root in politics and economics.

The grandchild of a slave, spiritual guide, and theologian, Howard Thurman knew the significance of the prophetic spirit to challenge injustice and give oppressed people a sense of hope and self-worth in an adversarial environment. A mystic, like Samuel from childhood, who never grew out of a sense of God's immediate presence, Thurman believed that the mystic's profound encounter with God affects the totality of their life. Filled with a sense of divine intimacy, welling up from their very soul, the mystic experiences something of the divine in everyone and works to create a world in which everyone can experience divinity as their deepest reality. Mystical experience is prophetic experience, according to Thurman. "Social action, therefore, is an expression of resistance against whatever tends to, or separates one, from the experience of God, who is the ground of his being."[19] Prophetic mysticism "has to do with the removal of all that prevents God from coming to himself in the life of the individual. Whatever there is that blocks this, calls for action."[20]

Resistance to injustice, like Moses' quest to liberate his people from the prison of racial and economic injustice, "is sacramental, because it is not an end in itself. Always, it is the individual who must be addressed, located, and released, underneath his misery and his hunger and his destitution. That whatever may be blocking his way to his own center where his altar may be found, this must be removed."[21] Prophetic challenge, for Thurman, must aim at the healing of both the oppressor and oppressed. Despite their wealth and power, the rich and famous, the powerful and privileged, may be alienated from their deepest selves, due to their failure to hear the cries of the poor. Their apathy has shut down their spirits and may lead, as Amos warns, to a famine of hearing God's word despite the technology of their megachurches and well-rehearsed praise

---

19   Howard Thurman, "Mysticism and Social Action: Lawrence Lectures and Discussions with Dr. Howard Thurman (London: International Association for Religious Freedom, 2014), Kindle Location, Kindle location, 235-236.

20   Ibid., Kindle location, 244-245.

21   Ibid., Kindle location, 249-251.

songs. The wealthy and powerful can gain the world, as Jesus says, and lose their souls, caught up in consumerism, power, entitlement, and self-gratification. As pastor-activist Michael-Ray Mathews asserts, white supremacy harms the souls of white people. Thurman believed that as dangerous as they are, political leaders who spew hate and promote chaos and alienation are to be pitied as well as opposed. Bravado and boasting often hide anxiety, insecurity, envy, and spiritual emptiness. Powerful and powerless alike need divine healing and this can only occur through the interplay of protest and reconciliation.

Prophetic challenge can be painful for those who have perpetuated injustice. They must see the negative impact of their actions on those who suffer. In Thurman's language, they may need to be "shocked" out of their complacency, sense of entitlement, and assumption of privilege and superiority. The goal of experiences of "shock" through protest, picketing, and boycotts is to awaken those who perpetrate injustice to their connection with those whom they knowingly or unknowingly harm. According to Thurman,

> What is important for the mystic is that the purpose of the shock treatment is to hold before the offender a mirror that registers an image of himself, that reflects the image of those who suffer at his hands. The total function of such action is to tear men from any alignments that prevent them from putting themselves in the other person's place, but it must never be forgotten that the central concern of the mystic is to seek to remove anything that prevents the individual from free and easy access to his own altar-stair that is in his own heart.[22]

Shocked out of their complacency and privilege – and sometimes unintentional injustice– the oppressor is given the opportunity to reclaim her or his own soul and discover her or his solidarity with all creation in God's beloved community. As unlikely as repentance may be among persons of power and privilege – and Amos quite realistically fears that change is unlikely among the rich and powerful of the Northern Kingdom! - healing

22   Ibid., Kindle location, 270-274.

of the oppressor becomes a catalyst for the embodiment of God's vision of Shalom in daily political and business decision-making.[23]

Ultimately, the Hebraic prophets – like today's mystics – see their relationship with God as both problem and hope. Injustice and idolatry reflect our turning from God to the devices and desires of our own hearts, whether these involve focus on shareholder profit apart from social and environmental responsibility, unjust protection of racial and gender privilege, political power, and the promotion of incivility and social division, and materialism and consumerism. Healing the soul of the nation – whether Israel, Judah, or the United States – requires a return to spiritual values and human-heartedness, and this will mean confession, repentance, and reparation. In the pluralistic environment of our current American ethos, this means affirming persons over profit, justice over privilege, compassion over power, and the health of future human and non-human generations over short-term financial and political gain. The prophets call us to become large souled persons, persons of spiritual stature, who see our wellbeing as part of an intricate fabric of destiny in which our wellbeing and the wellbeing of the planet are intimately connection. They remind us that in letting go of privilege and power, we reclaim our souls.

LISTENING TO THE VOICE OF THE PROPHET AMOS

If "God is still speaking," then we can affirm that God is speaking to us. There is a democracy of revelation such that even the non-human world experiences God.

Spiritual practice. Although the focus of this text is Amos, I have chosen to focus on Samuel's call because it describes more graphically the divine-human encounter than Amos' brief description of God's invitation to claim his prophetic vocation. It also

---

23 For more on Thurman's prophetic vision, see Bruce Epperly, *Prophetic Healing: Howard Thurman's Vision of Contemplative Activism* (Richmond: Friends United Press, 2020) and *The Work of Christmas: The Twelve Days of Christmas with Howard Thurman* (Vestal, NY: Anamchara Books, 2017).

mirrors some of our own experiences of encountering the Holy and receiving a vocation. Begin this exercise with silence, and then respond in the stillness with the words, "Speak God, your servant is listening." Then meditatively read the call of Samuel:

> Now the boy Samuel was ministering to the LORD under Eli. The word of the LORD was rare in those days; visions were not widespread. At that time Eli, whose eyesight had begun to grow dim so that he could not see, was lying down in his room; the lamp of God had not yet gone out, and Samuel was lying down in the temple of the LORD, where the ark of God was. Then the LORD called, "Samuel! Samuel!" and he said, "Here I am!" and ran to Eli, and said, "Here I am, for you called me." But he said, "I did not call; lie down again." So he went and lay down. The LORD called again, "Samuel!" Samuel got up and went to Eli, and said, "Here I am, for you called me." But he said, "I did not call, my son; lie down again." Now Samuel did not yet know the LORD, and the word of the LORD had not yet been revealed to him. The LORD called Samuel again, a third time. And he got up and went to Eli, and said, "Here I am, for you called me." Then Eli perceived that the LORD was calling the boy. Therefore Eli said to Samuel, "Go, lie down; and if he calls you, you shall say, 'Speak, LORD, for your servant is listening.'" So Samuel went and lay down in his place. Now the LORD came and stood there, calling as before, "Samuel! Samuel!" And Samuel said, "Speak, for your servant is listening." (I Samuel 2:1-10)

Reflecting on this passage, what words, images, music, or themes come to mind? What is the meaning of the responses for your life today, as an individual and citizen? What actions might your response inspire?

Take time throughout the days ahead to ask, "Speak, God, your servant is listening" and open to places where God may be addressing you in thoughts, emotions, challenges to action, or synchronous encounters. Chart any places where you might have "heard" God's voice.

QUESTIONS FOR REFLECTION

1) What do you think of the phrase "we are all mystics?" Have you ever had what you consider a mystical or self-transcendent experience or a sense of oneness, a paranormal experience, a feeling of another's feelings? How did you respond?

2) How might you respond if you, like Samuel, heard a strange voice in the night? How would you know that it came from God?

3) What is your response to the experiences of Martin Luther King and Thomas Merton? Have you felt anything similar?

4) Prophetic experiences join the Infinity of God with Finite History. What aspects of our lives and nation might the Infinite wish to address? What would it be like to hear the word of a prophet? What might a prophet say to us in America?

5) Walter Brueggemann speaks of the prophet as one who shares an alternative vision to the current unjust power structure. With what alternative vision might a contemporary prophet confront the United States? How might life be different in the USA if we followed the voices of the prophets?

6) Abraham Joshua Heschel speaks of the "Divine Pathos," God's passionate quest for justice, God's deep empathy and experience of the pain of the vulnerable and oppressed. What do you think of the idea that God feels our pain and is changed by God's experience of the world? Do you think God feels your feelings of joy and sorrow? Do you think God responds?

7) The Hebraic prophets tend to challenge the wealthy and powerful rather than call the poor to protest and rise up. Why do you think the prophets focus on the elite and powerful rather than the poor and powerless? What words might the prophets say to the dispossessed in the Northern Kingdom and the United States?

8) Who do you consider prophets in our time? What seems to be the common thread of their prophetic messages?

9) Do you think children, youth, and non-humans can be mystics and prophets? What prophetic voices have you experienced from children and youth?

Prayer. Still speaking God, open my senses that I might experience you in my day-to-day experiences and the politics of the nation. Give me an open spirit to your presence. Speak, God, your servant is listening. Show me the way and I will respond. Amen.

CHAPTER THREE

WHO IS THIS PROPHET?

I am no prophet, nor a prophet's son …
the Lord took me from following the flock,
and the Lord said to me,
"Go, prophesy to my people Israel."
(Amos 7:14-15)

Prophets seldom create personality cults. They don't want to be celebrities. In fact, they don't want to be in the limelight, nor frankly do they seek out the vocation of prophetic ministry. Prophetic ministry is often dangerous, divisive, and destructive to the prophet's reputation. Prophets are viewed with suspicion and often judged as disloyal, and as traitors, to their nation's values. They puncture our nationalistic pride and challenge the assumptions we have about our nation's values.

Prophets are also poetic and imaginative orators whose speeches blend dystopian and utopian images. Empathetic in spirit, they experience the harsh realities of injustice and poverty. They hear the cries of children, including the millions of American children who fall below the poverty line through no fault of their own, except perhaps the neglect and heartlessness of the powerful and wealthy. Their heart aches with the hopelessness of parents, unable to escape the cycle of poverty or having been plunged into destitution by unemployment, civil strife, or environmental disaster. They rail against state laws that require women and children to carry to term fetuses whose conception is the result of rape or incest, without requiring paternal support or pre-natal citizenship for every child who is conceived.

Prophets tell about what they see. They may seem over the top in their threats and invocation of divine anger, but this is the hyperbole of poetry and the anguish of empathy. Amos is often dramatic, even brutal, in his depictions of the terrors that await wayward nations and their leadership. Amos may even embellish images of divine anger and destruction and conflate his own anger with God's. Yet the alternative visions cast by the prophetic imagination are aimed at waking us up from the dream of peace and prosperity when the nightmare of national disaster is on the horizon as a result of our greed and oppression.

Amos saw and then he spoke, not about himself but about the dangers of injustice and God's stake in healing the nation. Like most of the biblical prophets, we know little about Amos' identity other than his domestic profession, prophetic call, and the time of his travel to the Northern Kingdom. The rest of his life is a mystery. I have several questions I would like to ask the prophet of Tekoa. I would love to know what led him to experience the Holy One, and then the nature of his decision-making process to leave the security of his home in Tekoa to cross the border to the Northern Kingdom, where he found shelter in the Northern Kingdom, and the shape of his life after returning home. Did he accept the call wholeheartedly or did he initially resist God's demands? Did he deliberate before venturing to the Northern Kingdom, knowing that he might be risking both life and livelihood? Given the close multi-generational and multi-family ties characteristic of his cultural context, how did he explain his decision to his family, and what was their response? Did he have friends and relations in the Northern Kingdom, who would provide shelter during his prophetic mission? Did he return home to a quiet retirement, or did he turn his attention to the injustices in the Southern Kingdom?

The book of Amos describes the prophet – in "Dragnet's" Joe Friday "just the facts ma'am" fashion - with these words.

> The words of Amos, who was among the shepherds of Tekoa, which he saw concerning Israel in the days of King Uzziah of Judah and in the days of Jeroboam son of Joash of Israel, two years before the earthquake. (Amos 1:1-2)

In response to being challenged by Amaziah, the priest of the holy place Bethel, who accused Amos of undermining King Jeroboam's rule, challenging him to go back where he came from in the South, Amos cites his outsider status:

> I am no prophet, nor a prophet's son; but I am a herds-man, and a dresser of sycamore trees, and the Lord took me from following the flock, and the Lord said to me, "Go, proph-esy to my people Israel." (Amos 7:14-15)

As I noted earlier, we don't know anything about Amos' family life or marital status and are given virtually no information about this economic situation. Many contemporary scholars believe that Amos was an economically comfortable shepherd-farmer, living in Judah, in Tekoa, approximately ten miles from Jerusalem, and just a short distance from Bethlehem. Established in his community and perhaps a member of a sheep breeders' cooperative, Amos was called by God to take a sabbatical – we don't know how long – from his occupational duties to emigrate northward to challenge the wealthy and powerful of the Northern Kingdom. Amos is also described as a "dresser," most likely an orchard owner, of sycamores, a type of fig tree whose fruit served to nourish both humans and animals. Some scholars believe that a more accurate translation is a "scratcher of sycamores," one who scraped or pierced the sour unripe fruit to promote the sweetness essential for the human pal-ate. Perhaps Amos was also a landowner who supplied food both to livestock and to the most vulnerable citizens of Judah, for whom these figs were a delicacy. He may also have supplied sheep to the Jerusalem Temple.

Amos had the economic freedom we suspect, to leave his flocks and orchards under the care of others during his prophetic sojourn. No doubt Amos was seen both as kin and as an outsider as Northerners and Southerners might have viewed each other in the aftermath of the Civil War. They had a common identity as children of Israel, but the ten northern tribes, known as Israel, had revolted due to the impact of political and economic differ-

ences around 930 BCE, approximately seventy years before Amos'
sojourn from Judah, the Southern Kingdom, to the Northern Kingdom, Israel.

We do know that Amos denied one title his opponents gave
to him. While obviously well-educated and spiritually inclined,
Amos was not a professional priest or prophet. His training in
theology and scripture was as a layperson and not a rabbi or priest.
Amos believed that his outsider status freed him from the professional limitations and economic dependency of "ordained" spiritual
leaders as well as their need to ensure the institutional survival of
the temples they led by promoting the interests of the king and
economic elite.

The biblical text notes that Amos' call to prophetic ministry
occurred two years before the great earthquake, dated in the vicinity
of 860-850 BCE. While the Book of Amos gives no information
about the length of Amos' prophetic ministry in the Northern
Kingdom, it suggests that some of his oracles were given during
the Fall Harvest Festival. We are given no information about what
happened to the prophet if – or after – he returned home.

Scholars suggest that the text we have today may be, like many
other biblical writings, the composition of several editors, inspired
by Amos' prophetic words, and perhaps spanning a period from
Amos' prophetic ministry to the overrunning of the Northern
Kingdom by Assyria thirty to forty years later. Some believe the
hopeful words that conclude the Book of Amos might have been
written after the fall of Assyria. It is clear from the text we have
today that, in addition to being a mystic, Amos was likely literate
and articulate, able to convey his message forcefully to the rich and
powerful of the Northern Kingdom.

We can conjecture that in midlife, perhaps settled in business
with a family, Amos had a life-transforming mystical experience
in which God spoke to him in words and images. In the biblical
tradition, encounters with God carry with them both a vocation
and mission. While Amos does not report a dramatic experience
like that of Isaiah's vision (Isaiah 6:1-8), approximately two decades

later, in which Isaiah experienced the Divine One, surrounded by angels and enthroned in the Jerusalem Temple, we can imagine that Amos, like Isaiah, heard a version of the question, "Whom shall we send?" and responded with fear and trembling, "Send me."

Amos' mystical experience appears to have been visual, auditory, and inspirational in nature. Though a layperson, and not part of a prophetic or clerical community, Amos experiences God as an intimate and forceful presence, and then describes Israel's present and future, revealing God's call to national repentance. He is not a soothsayer, able to give a clear and precise description of Israel's future. He is, however, able to ascertain what will occur if the business and political practices that widen the gap between the rich and poor continue in Israel. While the prophet spoke to the nation, his words are directly aimed at the religious and political elite of every age: the power brokers and economic moguls, the Wall Street, agribusiness, financial, and political sector of his and our time.

Amos had a specific sensitivity to the cries of the poor. Perhaps he experienced God's own anguish – and anger – at the injustices that led to poverty and homelessness in the Northern Kingdom. As a landowner, he might have been scandalized by farm foreclosures, orchestrated by the urban elite. Like our own time, much of the personal distress felt by the marginalized was intentionally created by the wealthy and powerful, the result of what today is called white collar crime, evident in unfair, predatory, dishonest, and manipulative business practices. Confronted with a God's eye view on injustice, and sensitive to the Divine pathos, Amos had no choice but to challenge the rich and powerful to confession and transformation. Like the author of the Epistle of James centuries later, Amos believed that faith without works is dead and that elaborate worship is spiritually deadening if it neglects responding to the cries of the poor.

LISTENING TO THE VOICE OF THE PROPHET AMOS

Charles Sheldon's social gospel classic *In His Steps* describes a small group of people who decide to ask themselves "what would Jesus do?" in their business, political, and personal decision-making. They believed that if persons ask for divine guidance, they will receive answers, albeit sometimes ambiguous and challenging, related to their life situations.

Spiritual Practice. In your own spiritual experiment, make a commitment to regularly ask "what would Jesus do?" or "whom would Amos challenge?" in your personal and professional decision-making as well as in your role as a citizen. Be observant of the paths that lie before you and any signs of divine guidance whether in terms of synchronous encounters, insights, intuitions, or moments of moral clarity. Be mindful of the values that shape your decisions. Are they in synch with God's vision for your life and citizenship? Will following Jesus' way or living in the spirit of Amos have an impact on your business or political involvement? What sacrifices will you need to make to be aligned with prophetic and gospel living?

QUESTIONS FOR REFLECTION

1) Do you believe that God calls people to challenge their nation's economic and national priorities? Once again, who are our current prophets? Who is making "good trouble," as John Lewis counsels, for those in power? How are they received by those in power?

2) Do the experiences of the biblical characters have any relevance to persons like ourselves, living under very different circumstances in terms of economic structures, political institutions, and technology? If so, what is their relevance?

3) How would you respond if you had a palpable sense of God's call in your life? Would you be willing to leave the comforts of your life to follow God's call to confront the rich and powerful?

4) In what areas are you following what you perceive to be God's call in your life today? Will following God's call require you to alter your lifestyle?

5) Taking some time for imaginative reflection, consider Amos' life following his prophetic emigration to the Northern Kingdom. What might have he done in the rest of his life? How might his professional life have changed as a result of his prophetic sojourn?

6) Why are prophets often viewed as disloyal to their nation? Is this judgment accurate? In our time, have prophets been viewed as disloyal and anti-American?

Prayer. Loving Parent of All, help me to be attentive to your still, small voice. Thank you for sending prophets throughout history and to our nation. Help me to listen for the words of prophets in our world today. Help me to believe that you are speaking within the events of my life as well as my personal experience. Help me to listen and respond and attune myself to your moral and spiritual arc in my life and the world. Amen.

CHAPTER FOUR

WHY BOTHER TO READ AMOS AT ALL?

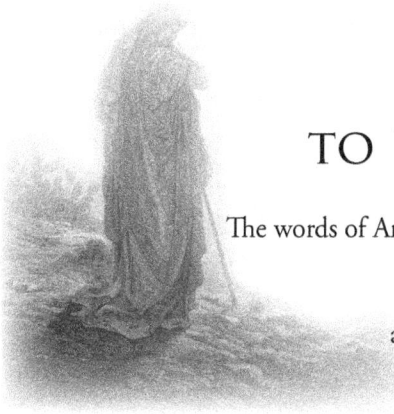

The words of Amos, who was among the shepherds of Tekoa,
which he saw concerning Israel
in the days of King Uzziah of Judah
and in the days of King Jeroboam of Israel,
two years before the earthquake.
And God said ... (Amos 1:1-2a)

As I noted earlier, this text is the result of a moment of inspiration, a sense that Something or Someone was leading me to ponder the prophet Amos in terms of my life as an educated and privileged American citizen and how ancient words can speak to our current American crises of poverty, incivility, violence, racism, and climate change. Despite my sense of divine inspiration, someone might challenge me: "Why bother to study a religious figure who has been dead nearly three thousand years?" They might continue: "Frankly, why bother to study the Bible period? Isn't it an era piece, from a distant time, with little relevance to our world of technology, complicated international economics, and complex governmental institutions? What can a shepherd from Tekoa have to say to a world of social media and factory farms? Why subject yourself to Amos' fury when you can read a gripping mystery, edifying biography, or a consoling devotional text?"

If I'm honest, a clear answer to these questions is difficult to find. I'm not a fundamentalist, who believes that the Bible is the unchanging word of God, qualitatively different from any other spiritual text, revealing God's will perfectly and without error. Nor do I believe that when we read the bible, we can always interpret its meaning accurately in our time. Moreover, I believe that the Bible is one of many inspired spiritual texts. I also read the Bhagavad Gita and Upanishads, the Buddhist sutras, the Tao Te Ching, and the spiritual verses of Rumi and the First Americans. I experience inspiration in contemporary theology, science, psychology, and literature, and I enjoy an intricate and entertaining mystery, whether by Agatha Christie, Tony Hillerman, Louise Penny, or theologian Susan Thistlewaite! I also see the Bible as a timely and timebound book, like all religious texts, often reflecting the religious and ethical biases and limitations of the communities that produced this library of texts. Within the Bible, there are bloodthirsty and vindictive passages along with some of the most uplifting and inspiring passages, still capable of transforming lives, healing broken spirits, and inspiring the quest for justice. God is seen as the Great Lover, whose grace envelopes all of us. God is also seen – and in certain passages in Amos portrayed – as virtually unrelenting in divine judgment.

Perhaps that early morning divine inspiration came to me because I believe, despite Amos' images of a judgmental God, that Amos still speaks to our hunger for a better world. Beneath Amos' dystopian vision is a glimmer of hope for transformation and healing. Amos speaks to the conscience of America, challenging us to embody the American dream of liberty and justice for all. Amos' prophetic protest is motivated by empathy for the poor and rich alike, hoping against hope that they will be spared what seems to be inevitable destruction. My own life with scripture and the quest for a more just America has opened me to God's wisdom in the words of the shepherd from Tekoa. Amos challenges the wealthy and powerful to let their hearts be broken so that they and we can experience the suffering of the poor.

My willingness to say "yes" to the divine whisper emerged because I am appalled at the apparent neglect of prophetic religion in the United States. As I look at social media, I observe that virtually none of my friends and colleagues who describe themselves as orthodox, evangelical, or Bible-believing Christians take the message of the prophets seriously. They read the first two chapters of Genesis to challenge the theory of evolution and make a case for original sin, cherry pick a handful of passages in the first five books of the Bible as proof that God hates the LGBTQ community while neglecting the strictures against divorce, sing praise songs based on the Psalms, and they stretch the poetry of Jeremiah 1 and Psalm 139 to justify biblical prohibitions against abortion. But, when it comes to the prophets, they are silent, assuming the prophetic denunciation of profits ahead of people is irrelevant to 21st-century free market capitalism and that while, in their minds, the new covenant did not supersede prohibitions against homosexuality, it relativized prophetic criticism of unrestrained economics and the gap between the rich and the poor. My conservative Christian friends and their pastors have often preferred to focus on profits to the exclusion of the prophets! They have seen our nation's salvation dependent on the actions of prevaricating politicians, whom they perceive as God's instruments, despite their rage and incivility. They sometimes compare their anointed politicians to Amos even though their anointed politicians have virtually no sympathy for the poor, the stranger, or the marginalized, and fan the flames of xenophobia and division. To invoke the spirit of Amos' critique of unrestrained profit making and affirmation of the needs of the poor over unrestrained consumption leads to the accusation of being a socialist!

I have found that most conservative Christians are unknowingly "functional heretics," a term I seldom use, when it comes to taking the prophetic word seriously. They are theological descendants of the Marcionite emphasis on the New Testament as the primary Word of God and corresponding denunciation of the First or Old Testament as reflecting an inferior spirituality and legalism and its wrathful and earthy deity. Others read the Bible only through the lens of an evangelical understanding of the apostle Paul, seeing salvation as primarily individualistic and transactional in nature and separating the world into two kingdoms, the heavenly and the earthly, believing that the primary task of faith involves your personal relationship with Jesus and focusing on "heaven and how to get there" to the exclusion of any focus on righting the wrongs of social, economic, or racial injustice. Influenced by the

Lutheran theology of two kingdoms, sacred and secular, Christian ethics came to mean that the individual Christian is challenged to live a life of sacrifice in their personal relationships, while the Christian as citizen and economic leader is free to focus on power and profit. What is forbidden in individual ethics, violence, and greed, is often seen as a necessity in institutional, economic, and national policy and political involvement.

Entranced by American individualism and economics, many North American Christians fail to see that Jesus and James as well as Paul were profoundly influenced by the communal and social ethic of the Hebraic scriptures. Jesus' first sermon, quoting Isaiah's good news to the poor and freedom to the captives (Luke 4:18-19), and the Sermon on the Mount (Matthew, chapters 5-7) are rooted in prophetic spirituality. Paul's urging of Philemon to liberate his slave Onesimus as an affirmation of their equality in terms of God's grace transcends individualistic and transactional understandings of spirituality and salvation and joins the Epistle of James in asserting that faith without works is dead. If people are equals before God, as Paul says to Philemon, they must have equality in social and economic relationships. What would have happened in the course of Christian history if Christians had read Paul's liberating words from Philemon instead of proof-texting the demeaning counsel, "slaves obey your masters?" (Ephesians 6:5).

In reading the prophets, we rescue the bible and, dare we say, Christianity from the hypnotic power of individualism, consumerism, racism, and unrestrained and amoral free market capitalism. For the prophets, the excuse, "it's not personal, just business," is a sham. Everything is personal to the prophets. Any act that diminishes human value, sacrificing the vulnerable for profit-making, is an affront to the Creator. In reading the prophets, we also reclaim the importance of economic and ecological justice in our quest for salvation wholeness.

Why Read the Bible at All? As a child, growing up in a small town evangelical church, I regularly joined my Sunday School classmates in singing "The B-I-B-L-E, oh that's the book for me,

I stand alone on the word of God, the B-I-B-L-E." I also remember bumper stickers pronouncing, "The Bible says it. I believe it. And that settles it." These affirmations were supposed to convince Christians and non-Christians alike of biblical authority. Today's biblical literalists believe that the bible is authoritative and accurate in every detail because, in their reading of scripture, the bible says that it is inerrant and authoritative, whether we are speaking of the age of the earth, homosexuality, the apparent justification of slavery, or the role of women in the church. They cite as clear proof of authority and inerrancy a passage from I Timothy 3:16, "All scripture is inspired [God breathed] by God and is useful for teaching, for reproof, for correction, and for training in righteousness."

As you consider the nature of biblical inspiration, notice the word is "inspired" not "inerrant." Inspiration can transform lives even if it is found in poetry, literature, or music, and not provable as literal fact! Inspiration is about imagination and the presentation of alternative ways of looking at our lives and the world and not a circular argument persuasive only to "true believers."

Further, at the time Timothy was written in the latter part of the first century, the New Testament as canon did not exist. The early Christians initially had only the stories of Jesus and the Hebraic scriptures to guide them. Only the First or Old Testament, if we take Timothy's text literally, is inspired. Moreover, an inerrant, unchanging text is locked in the past. The biblical text, from the literalist perspective, has only one meaning, the original intent of the timeless divine author, whereas an inspired word evolves and changes as historical, scientific, medical, and political situations change. Literal readings of scripture imprison us in the past and justify the status quo. They lack the poetry and artistry of the imagination, the connection of concrete reality with life-changing possibility.

Today, of course, many readers, including those raised in conservative churches from which they've migrated, struggle to see inspiration in passages that describe genocide, mass murder, and death sentences for moral misdemeanors as acts commanded by God. For them, there is little good news in scripture. The seeds of grace have been choked by the weeds of fundamentalism. These refugees from the church, along with the growing number of "nones," persons without any religious identification, are put off by a biblicism that inspires, from their perspective, misogyny, racism, homophobia, scientific skepticism, abandonment of the environment, and opposition to masks and vaccines.

Still, I believe that we can read scripture with heart as well as mind, seeing scripture like prophetic experience, and our own experiences of the Holy, as the interplay of divine inspiration, human experience, and historical context. Divine revelation does not eliminate human insight, limitation, and fallibility but awakens us to larger visions of the universe and the spiritual and moral arcs of history. Divine revelation helps us to see ourselves more clearly, waking us up to sin, grace, and responsibility.

I believe that the library of books that make up scripture can be read in light of an expanded version of the Wesleyan Quadrilateral which finds authority in the interplay of the words of scripture itself, human reason and ethical reflection, religious experience, and moments of self-transcendence, and two thousand years of Christian theology, supplemented with the wisdom of science, culture, current events, environmental science and critical race theories, and the insights of other religions as well as the questions of agnostics and atheists. Yes, even the questions of non-believers – the "so what" and "do you really believe God did that" questions – are fertile ground for understanding the divine inspiration we see in scripture!

A Good Enough Bible? When I was a young parent, anxious to do the right thing in raising our only child, I came upon the counsel "be a good enough parent." This advice noted that we cannot expect to be perfect parents, knowing all the right things to do and always responding with calm and insight to our children's issues, but we can be good enough to give them roots and wings, and a strong foundation for their personal adventures. I believe we can find insight in a "good enough" Bible, or Quran or Upanishads, not perfect or error-free or always morally coherent, but filled with insights and guidance for a life of faith, ethical commitment, and spiritual growth.

I believe that our understanding of the bible reflects our view of the interplay of divine and human inspiration and authority. Authoritarian views of scripture reflect images of God as absolute sovereign, supernaturally active in the world bypassing the regularities of nature and separating persons into siloes of saved and unsaved based on divine decision or adherence to doctrinal orthodoxy. Fundamentalist and authoritarian views of scripture are by nature binary in spirit and action in their clear separation of truth and falsehood. From this perspective, scripture is unique and discontinuous with human experience, preserved from all error, and subject to only one interpretation. Asking questions of scripture is discouraged. Any other interpretation than a clear literal understanding is false and leads to spiritual darkness and eternal damnation.

In contrast, I believe that a relational and dynamic understanding of divine revelation suggests that scriptural authority emerges from the interplay of lively and ongoing divine inspiration and human experience. Revelation is universal and yet always personal and intimate. All creatures are inspired by God who is always speaking a personal word to each person and culture. Deep down, all of us are mystics, touched by God, even if we are unaware of it. Scripture emerges from awareness of the Holy and reflection on life-changing experiences of God's presence. Recognizing the historical and finite nature of humankind's experience of revelation, faithfulness to scripture means challenging certain passages while framing your life around others.

In terms of prophetic inspiration, while everyone experiences God, I believe Amos uniquely encountered the divine. In the spirit of Celtic thin places, transparent to the Holy, Amos was personally touched by God and said "yes" to God's experiential and vocational call. In the spirit of Eric Liddell from "Chariots of Fire," Amos might declare, "God made me a prophet, and when I speak for the vulnerable, I can feel God's passion." Finite and fallible, Amos and the prophets channeled God's word to their unique historical context. An often-angry artist and poet, Amos mirrored the divine anger at injustice. Harsh words, yet they are motivated by love and the desire for the nation to escape the horrific possibilities of the future. As we prayerfully contemplate the words of Amos, we discover that they still resound whenever we perceive injustice, oppression, and economic manipulation. Amos still has a word for us in our own political and economic context.

Accordingly, we can affirm biblical inspiration and say, without equivocation, that God was present in Amos' mystical experience and the message that emerged from it. Not all-inclusive or infallible, Amos' words and personality reflected God's call to social transformation and God's preferential option for the poor. The power of Amos' words is their blending of universal insight, applicable to all times and places, with the prophet's own 8th century BCE historical and political context. They echo across the centuries calling into question every institution that puts power and profit ahead of personal wellbeing. Amos intends to mediate an alternative divine vision, a provocative divine possibility, that will change the lives of everyone who truly hears and responds to his messages. Amos wonders if the leaders of the Northern Kingdom can truly hear God's voice, mired as they are in self-interest and exceptionalism. He believes that his message offers the nation one last chance. God's word and God's vision moving through and shaped by his words can transform lives. As we find ourselves 2800 years later facing our own economic and environmental precipice, Amos warns us of the consequences of complacency and apathy, of dishonesty and disregard, and yet holds out hope that perhaps we might change our ways and avert the disaster on the horizon.

The power of the prophetic books, and the Book of Amos, is their challenge to experience the world prophetically. To see the world with God's eyes. To feel God's pain and joy. To become sensitive to the divine currents moving through the daily news and to always be dissatisfied with your personal as well as national morality. Reading scripture prophetically does not eliminate error or imperfection in the reader's responses. The prophets were clear, even when they were most adamant in critiquing the sinfulness of political and economic power brokers, that they too fell under God's judgment. They too had lives of privilege and struggled to put God first in their lives. Their own humility enabled them, even as prophets like Amos "damned" their nation and its political, economic, and political leaders, to see common ground with their opponents and pray that their opponents might escape the judgment to come.

We can read the prophets' words and act prophetically, cognizant of our own limitations and biases. Humble reading enables us to care for those whom we challenge. It also prevents us from succumbing to the violence and incivility that we see in those whose policies and lifestyles we challenge.

A good enough Bible provides a way through the wilderness. Inspired and inspiring, it enlightens us to injustice and our complicity in the pain of others. It also challenges us to take our place as God's companions, faithful and fallible, in healing the earth.

We are writing our own "bibles" today in our protesting injustice and witnessing to God's presence moving through diverse forms of human and non-human experience. Seeking healing amid challenge and transformation amid critique, the prophet, like scripture at its best, is inspired by love of rich and poor alike, so that all can experience a feast and not a famine of hearing God's word.

LISTENING TO THE PROPHET AMOS

We can experience the prophetic imagination that inspired Amos. We can discern God's voice in the cries of the poor, and God's passion for justice in our own critique and resistance to the powers and principalities that perpetuate injustice, racism, and planetary destruction.

Spiritual Practice. After a time of quiet openness to God's wisdom and challenge, meditatively read Jesus' first sermon (Luke 4:18-19), based on the words of the prophet Isaiah (Isaiah 61:1):

> The Spirit of the Lord is upon me,
>> because he has anointed me
>> to bring good news to the poor.
> He has sent me to proclaim release to the captives
>> and recovery of sight to the blind,
> to let the oppressed go free,
>> to proclaim the year of the Lord's favor.

What words or images come to you as you reflect on this passage? How might this passage challenge your values? How might this passage challenge our nation's values? How might this shape legislation if voters and legislators truly took Jesus' and Isaiah's words seriously?

QUESTIONS FOR REFLECTION

1) How do you understand the authority of scripture? What are the challenges of reading scripture?

2) What parts of scripture are most meaningful to you? What parts of scripture are most problematic to you?

3) What are your other sources of inspiration and spiritual guidance, outside of scripture?

4) Why do you think many American Christians relegate the prophetic writings to the spiritual and inspirational sidelines?

5) What do you think of the idea that our understandings of biblical authority – fundamentalist, inerrant, inspirational but fallible – shape our understandings of politics and pluralism, the recognition of different paths to truth?

6) Do you think Christians and other persons of faith can learn from agnostics and atheists? In what ways can their critiques deepen our faith?

7) What do you think of the notion of a "good enough" Bible?

Prayer. Let the words of scripture in their wondrous fallibility awaken me to your presence in my life and your vision of Shalom for our nation. Let me listen to the prophets and mystics in scripture. Let me listen to the teachings of Jesus. Help me to see the wisdom of scripture as well as its imperfections that I might find scripture to be a spiritual guidepost in the wilderness of contemporary political life. Amen.

CHAPTER FIVE

YOU ARE NOT THAT EXCEPTIONAL!

(Amos, Chapters 1 and 2)

The Lord roars from Zion,
and utters the divine voice from Jerusalem. (1:2)

The Book of Amos and Amos the 8th century BCE prophet challenge our concepts of God and mysticism. Amos is a mystic, who has a direct and life-changing encounter with God and a series of visionary and auditory experiences in which he discerns God's vision of history and the fate of an unrepentant nation. God is real for him, and while Amos may always have had a Godward orientation, his encounter with the Holy One, not unlike the younger Isaiah's vision of God in the Jerusalem Temple, agitated the comfortable shepherd so greatly that he felt compelled to be God's passionate messenger to the powerful, perhaps even to people like himself, who had a stake in the maintenance of the status quo, despite its foundations in economic injustice and the dehumanization of its most vulnerable fellow citizens. Amos knew the centers of power and although he does not discourage protest from the poor, the prophet knows that meaningful change will not happen without a radical reorientation in the attitudes and policies of the powerful. Unless the powerful and affluent – people like himself - confess and repent their unjust ways, the nation will be doomed.

For those who believe that mystical encounters give you a perpetual smile, promote a sense of calm, ensure economic prosperity, and lead to abandoning the complexities of politics and economics, the prophet Amos will seem the spiritual inferior to Gautama the

Buddha and the Taoist ancient Lao Tzu, both of whom abandoned politics to foster a sense of peace and equanimity and whose religious descendants until recently counseled disengagement from society.[24] Amos' passionate message emerges from a spirituality that is far different from the stereotypical Christian monastic gently and quietly devoting themselves to prayer, smiling affably to all whom they encounter, "content to let the world go by, to know no gain or loss."[25]

Spirituality takes many forms, some more contemplative, others more activist. Amos hears the cries of the poor knows that every day brings gain to the wealthy and loss to the poor, and that must change – now! While we must honor the pathways of Gautama and Lao Tzu, as well as the contemplative Christian monastic tradition, Amos' spiritual stature comes from his empathetic attachment to the suffering of the marginalized and oppressed. This world matters. Housing and diet matter. Economic instability and disparity matter. Amos discovers that God is more interested in justice in the marketplace and the judicial system than in spiritual equanimity. Enlightenment, wholeness, is found in the scrum of political and institutional intrigue for the shepherd of Tekoa and the God he follows.

Amos defies our mystical stereotypes, reminding us that not all mystics are calm and collected or avoid conflict. In my *Mystics in Action: Twelve Saints for Today*, I discuss contemporary mystics such as Dorothy Day, Simone Weil, and Dag Hammarskjold, who broke the mystical mold to confront injustice.[26] To our consternation, some of the most insightful mystics smoked, drank, swore, and employed righteous anger to confront injustice. They were on occasion passionate and irascible, and reflected God's own passionate quest for justice. Amos may have had a calm spiritual

---

24   Today, Buddhist mystics and spiritual guides such as Thich Nhat Hanh counsel engaged Buddhism, which involves both contemplation and activism, to transform society and secure justice for the downtrodden.

25   Elizabeth Clephane, "Beneath the Cross of Jesus."

26   Bruce Epperly, *Mystics in Action: Twelve Saints for Today* (Maryknoll, NY: Orbis Books, 2020).

center, born of his encounter with God, but bursting forth from that center was a mighty voice for justice and social transformation reflecting God's passionate confrontation with him. The shepherd, or sheep breeder, from Tekoa revealed the divine message he received, and it was divine anger at injustice and poverty, for the most part, caused by the decisions of the wealthy and powerful.

Amos' God is also disappointing to those who see God as primarily gentle and mild, apathetic, unbiased, and passive in relationship to the problems of the world as well as those who believe God creates the world and then sits at the sidelines unrelated to the historical process, leaving history and politics solely to human actors. The perfection of Amos' God is not found in changelessness or constant joy, but in dynamic relatedness and embeddedness in the delight and tragedy of life. God is passionately involved in history, and God takes sides in the historical process. While God may love all God's children, the God Amos depicts sides with the vulnerable and marginalized, the forgotten and objectified, the "nuisances and nobodies" of the world.[27] In the poetry of protest, Amos reveals God as all too human in God's passion to jar us into becoming fully human, imitating God in our quest for justice.

Although God condemns their economic and religious practices, God does not abandon the wealthy and apathetic oppressors. The Holy One recognizes that their healing requires spiritual, ethical, and economic transformation. Unless the affluent and powerful awaken to the cries of the poor, their elaborate worship celebrations will be prosecuting witnesses revealing their spiritual malfeasance. To experience spiritual healing and personal deliverance, the wealthy and powerful must experience the heartbreak of recognizing their intentional or unintentional complicity in others' poverty. Without being shocked into wakefulness, they will experience a more deadly famine than the one that is devasting the most vulnerable members of the community, they will experience a famine of hearing the word of God.

---

27 "Nuisances and nobodies" is a term coined by biblical scholar John Domonic Crossan.

Amos the prophet and Amos' God intend to shock the wealthy and powerful. As Howard Thurman avers, the mystic's encounter with God inspires them to confront injustice and challenge anything that stands in the way of human wholeness. Prophetic anger is the prelude to prophetic healing in which the oppressor is awakened to an alternative vision of economics, repents of their injustice, and then seeks to make things right by repairing the damage they have done, sacrificing much of their privilege and power for the wellbeing of their destitute and desperate neighbors. Amos' God is a spiritual, economic, and political surgeon who must – in the spirit of Jesus' parable of the vine and branches – cut off all the limbs that bear the fruits of injustice. The cancer of economic injustice must be excised for the nation to survive. We may have to receive a heart transplant to be empathetic to the cries of the poor. The powerful and affluent must change their way of life to prevent any life-threatening reoccurrence.

Amos' Words of Doom. (1:1-2:3) Amos the prophet is a spiritual buzzkill. A mystical marauder, whose words agitate and condemn, and call for radical transformation. Amos is the physician, bearing news from the Great Physician, that our current lifestyle will lead to a premature and agonizing death. The physician Amos calls us to change, beginning today, if we are to avert our fate! Moreover, Amos, like many medical professionals, bears the burden of knowing that most of his intended audience will not change their ways, they are too invested in their current lifestyles – as in the case of medical admonitions related to our dietary and exercise habits - and cannot imagine anything different than the growing gap of wealthy and poor. They may even morally justify their wealth, connecting it with hard work and ingenuity in contrast to the laziness and dullness of the poor. Though the odds are against it, Amos recognizes, hoping against hope, that they will listen and, in so doing, avoid the consequences of their economic and lifestyle choices.

The Lion Roars. (1:2) American poet Emily Dickinson once counseled "tell all the truth but tell it slant," championing the viewpoint that dispensing truth is like prescribing medicine, suited for the listener, thus reducing their defensiveness, and giving them space to decide while preserving their self-respect. While Dickinson's counsel is often appropriate in personal and professional relationships and often works wonders in congregational life, this is not the way of Amos or the God of the Book of Amos. The house is on fire, death and destruction is imminent, and the occupants are asleep. Worse yet, those who are awake are adding fuel to the fire that will eventually destroy our homes. The alarm needs to blare, the occupants must be shocked into wakefulness if they are to escape disaster. The wealthy and powerful of the Northern Kingdom – and the urbanites of Jerusalem – need to be awakened from their comfortable complacency before it's too late.

The poor and homeless already see the handwriting on the wall, but there is little they can do to change their fate without the leadership of the economic elites. In fact, without an immediate response, it may already be too late for rich and poor alike!

God roars at the violence and injustice of nations and economic and political leaders. God is not tame, nor can God be domesticated by religion or nationalism. God's aim at Shalom must, in the case of the Northern Kingdom, take the form of turning everything familiar and predictable upside down. There will be environmental disasters. Weather patterns will be unpredictable. There will be famines, floods, and fires. There will be plagues. The earth will shake. Pestilence and virus will level communities. Enemies will rise to threaten national sovereignty. For Amos, these are divine calls to attention.

In contrast to the prophet's world view, I believe these catastrophes may *not* be the result of direct divine intervention but the outcome, in a divinely ordered world, of decisions that harm the earth and its inhabitants. Decisions that focus only on profit to the neglect of the working poor, the homeless, and the non-human world will lead to spiritual, environmental, and economic catastrophe. Eventually the shields the wealthy and powerful erect against "acts of God" will collapse and they too will suffer the consequences of their injustice. Acts have consequences that affect not only our spiritual lives but the environment.

Regardless of the source of disaster, divine punishment, or the impact of human behavior, the Lion God of Amos wants to get our attention. Wake up. Time is running out. This may be your last chance. The Lion God is like a parent snatching a child out of the way of an oncoming car. Passionate and angry at the child's foolishness, but more passionately loving the child, who is the parent's heart's desire. As angry as Amos' God may be, God's anger is righteous anger, inspired by love, and the reality that God can't fully be God if humankind destroys itself.

The Ignorance of Schadenfreude. (1:3-2:3) The word "schadenfreude" gained notoriety during the coronavirus pandemic as many of the vaccinated and masked felt a certain guilty and unspoken pleasure at hearing the growing statistics of illness and death among the unvaccinated and unmasked, the anti-vaxxers and Trumpers who refused simple health measures due to a simplistic understanding of freedom, the uninformed and manipulative counsel of political leaders, or uncritical acceptance of fake news. We might have thought "they're just getting what they deserve" as an apostle of anti-vaccination is hospitalized, ventilated, and dies a week after going to an anti-vaccine protest. "They should have known better. Now they are suffering the consequences of their stupidity. Thank God, I trust science and not the lies that they are fed!"

We are all in search of an "other," an inferior person who lacks our sophistication and ethical compass. We may gain pleasure from seeing ourselves as special and unique, awake in a world of darkness, chosen by God in a world of wayward nations. Despite the delight in comparing our deserved good fortune to the earned misfortunes of others, deep down we know that we are all in the same storm and that their pain and suffering threaten our own wellbeing. Perhaps, deep down, we recognize that we are not as good as we pretend to be.

The citizens of the Northern Kingdom must have felt a quiet delight as they heard Amos' divinely inspired words of doom heaped upon the states that surround them. Amos' "rhetoric of entrapment" lulled them into complacency before shocking them by its words of judgment and threat.

Though they perceived themselves as the apple of God's eyes, Israel's relationships with its neighbors were ambiguous at best and often warlike in practice. The children of Israel had sojourned from Egypt to the "promised land," then occupied Canaan by a process of assimilating, and then displacing or subjugating its native peoples. In securing and maintaining power, they slaughtered innocents at Jericho and did battle with their neighbors. A chosen people, the children of Israel and their descendants in the Southern and Northern Kingdoms saw themselves as moral and spiritual superiors to their neighbors. They also believed that their chosen status – their identity as God's beloved nation, or nations - exempted them from the judgments their neighbors were receiving.

The citizens of the Northern Kingdom and their Southern kin knew well the national sins of their neighbors. Some of them may have been inflicted against the Southern and Northern Kingdoms. Believing in their moral superiority and special status before God, Amos' audience may have nodded their heads, feeling quite good about themselves, as they heard Amos' poetry of condemnation of their neighbors for:

- ✓ Brutality aimed at defeated cities perpetrated by Damascus.
- ✓ Deportation of defeated enemies to labor camps in Edom, enacted by Gaza.
- ✓ Relocation of kin to labor camps in Edom, enacted by Tyre.
- ✓ Destruction and ongoing violence against kin, executed by Edom.
- ✓ Murder of non-combatants, including pregnant women, inflicted by Ammon.
- ✓ The desecration of the corpse of a defeated ruler, carried out by Moab.

The Northern Kingdom's neighbors had enacted brutal acts motivated by the nationalistic quest for security and wealth. No doubt, Israel's enemies, like most nations then and now, justified violence in foreign policy as the means to ensure national sovereignty and eliminate the military threat of their neighbors, including the threats posed by the Northern Kingdom. The Northern Kingdom's neighbors surely realized many economic benefits from their military incursions. For such brutality, they deserve to be punished without pity, so says Amos' God and so believes Amos' complacent audience. Neighboring nations and their leaders will experience divine retribution through divine, destructive "fire," devouring strongholds, destroying walls, laying to waste communities, and killing political leaders.

Perhaps, the military and economic leaders of the Northern Kingdom considered the positive benefits of such divine retribution just as the leaders of the United States and other nations have gained from other nations' military defeats and political insecurity. As a result of their neighbors' demise, the Northern Kingdom would be able to open new markets and annex new territories, thus ensuring economic growth and national security in terms of future threats from the Assyrian kingdom, currently dealing with opponents on its borders but more than capable of overwhelming the Northern Kingdom at any time. Decimated neighbors might provide a buffer for Assyrian aggression, thus enabling life to go on as usual, without any changes in lifestyle or economics on the part of Israel's ruling elite.

Closer to Home. (2:4-5) The economic and political elites feel a certain ethical smugness as they hear of the destruction of their neighbors. We are chosen – we are God's light, the recipients of an eternal covenant – this can't happen to us. Then, a shiver runs down their collective spines as Amos turns from historical enemies to pronounce divine condemnation on the Southern Kingdom, Judah, whose seat of power is the city of David, Jerusalem.

While the Northern and Southern Kingdoms may have had their own foreign policy and economic differences, Amos' indictment now focuses on Judah's relationship with God. At first glance, God's complaint against Judah appears to join faith and action at a personal and corporate level. Injustice is the fruit of idolatry, of worshipping false gods as a way of securing prosperity and comfort rather than following the ethical demands of the One True God.

> They have rejected the law of the LORD,
> and have not kept his statutes,
> but they have been led astray by the same lies
> after which their ancestors walked. (Amos 2:4)

We are not told what laws and statutes Judah has rejected. Perhaps, their transgressions involved lack of concern for the poor and economic injustice as well as failure to put God first in their lives. During the time of Solomon, the last successful king of the unified realm, symbols, and images from competing religious traditions were brought into David's holy city, challenging the peoples' faithfulness to Yahweh as the One and Only True God. To Amos and the God of Amos, loyalty to the gods of Canaan and Judah's neighbors jeopardized their commitment to the ways of Yahweh, the God of Exodus, the One who had chosen Israel, all twelve tribes, to be God's people.

The prophetic tradition connects infidelity to God with injustice and idolatry. Since our understanding of God's nature shapes our character and ethical decision-making, good theology, according to the prophets, epitomized by Israel's emerging tradition of ethical monotheism, leads to right action toward friend and foe alike. If you follow the One True God of Israel, then you will practice justice and hospitality to neighbor and stranger alike. On the whole, the prophets also believed that following the gods of the Canaanites, the gods of soil and vegetation, leads to ritualized sexual immorality, aimed at ensuring their god's support. Turning from the One True God, despite apparent short-term benefits in crop yields, will eventually lead to political, religious, and economic disaster.

As they heard the divine denunciation of Judah, their historic kin also chosen to be God's people, the listeners in Samaria, Bethel, and Gilgal may have begun to wonder if they too might be the subject of God's condemnation. "This is getting close to home," they might have murmured to one another. I suspect that they banished such negativity from their minds until Amos proclaimed that there is no exemption to the impact of divine justice on wrongdoers. Even the chosen ones must face the consequences of their actions. God "will send a fire on Judah and it shall devour the strongholds of Jerusalem." (Amos 2:5) Their sense of national indestructibility eroding, the Northern Kingdom's elite wonder if they might be next on the list of divine indictments.

You Are Not an Exception. (2:6-16) Israel saw itself as God's chosen people. God had liberated them from slavery, brought them out of Egypt, and provided them with a homeland, a land of milk and honey. While the Canaanites might have told a very different story about the occupation of Canaan, the children of Israel believed that, unlike the indigenous peoples of Canaan, they had special status before God. God will honor and protect them despite the constant threats from neighbors and superpowers. God will always forgive their wrongdoing and mitigate the consequences of their disobedience. The national myth described them as spiritually and ethically unique, far superior to their neighbors in faith and morality. Their own history of genocide, celebrated in their national myths, and internal economic unrest did not, in their minds, disqualify them from God's protection or special status among nations.

It must have come as a shock when they heard God's indictment of their nation. God lumped them together with inferior nations, putting both Israel, the Northern Kingdom, and Judah, on the same moral playing field as the enemies that surrounded them. Worse yet, their special status did not exempt them from divine punishment or the consequences of institutionalized economic injustice.

Perhaps, as they heard the indictment, many of the elite justified their behavior, "These are normal business practices. Isn't business about profit? There's nothing personal if our actions indirectly harm others. It's probably their fault anyway for living beyond their means and borrowing against their property. Some will succeed and others fail. If we let our economic guard down by being generous to everyone, our businesses would fail and the whole system will collapse. The poor are responsible for their fate. What can we do anyway? The poor are with us always!"

Then, perhaps a deeper truth came to them as Amos' words cascaded upon them like an ever-flowing stream: "To God, it's never just business, it's always personal. God weighs the pain of the poor against the comfort of the wealthy and powerful and judges them for the pain directly or indirectly caused by their business and political practices. You know what you're doing, and you better stop now, or else the whole house of cards will collapse."

The indictment is clear. Israel's political, religious, and economic elite is being held accountable for the following crimes against God's vision of Shalom, wholeness for all humankind:

✓ "Selling the righteous for silver and the needy for a pair of sandals," that is, putting people into involuntary servitude, debtor's prisons, or the equivalent of slave labor, for economic gain.

✓ "Trampling the head of the poor into the dust of the earth," that is, devastating the poor as if they are no better than the ground beneath their feet, lesser mortals, "different from us," worthy of no ethical or personal consideration.

✓ "Pushing the afflicted out of the way," putting the poor at the sidelines, getting ahead of them, and then snatching the necessities from the economically vulnerable to line their own pockets.

✓ "Father and son going into the same girl, and profaning God's holy name," objectifying and using women for their own pleasure, using their power and privilege to dominate women who may have had no ability to say "no" to their advances.

✓ "Laying themselves down beside every altar on garments taken in pledge," that is, gaining notoriety from their donations and endowments, funded by cheating the poor out of their property and benefiting by the impoverished farmers' inability to pay high-interest loans, despite the divine law prohibiting usury.

✓ "Drinking wine" and celebrating at religious festivals, funded by fines levied against the poor, create a cycle of indebtedness, by late payment fees.

Speaking for God and sharing the visions he witnessed, Amos makes a clear connection between greed and economic injustice and the eclipse of authentic religious experience and ethical standards in persons' daily lives and decision-making. Despite God's past liberating work and deliverance from the nation's enemies, the elite, prosperous, and powerful seek to silence any criticism of the social and economic order by:

✓ Muting the voice of the prophets when their protests challenge the nation's economics and politics.

✓ Compromising the moral integrity of the Nazarites, whose calling is to maintain ritual purity.

✓ Recognizing only religious voices that undergird and bless the current economic and political system by their promotion of a type of 8th Century BCE "prosperity gospel."

✓ Seeing religion's role as supporting the *status quo* as blessed by God and part of the natural order of things, thus promoting the viewpoint that God has no interest in social justice and the pain of the vulnerable and impoverished.

Recently biblical scholars have used the phrase "rent capitalism," taken from social anthropology, to describe the economic practices condemned by Amos. In socially sanctioned rent capitalism, peasant farmers produce their crops primarily for the purpose of feeding their families and take only small portions of their agricultural produce to market. Landowners or merchants purchase their remaining produce. These businesspeople make loans at high interest to the farmers during times of famine and weather instability. Taking out loans from Jerusalem merchants and property

owners places peasant farmers in a dependent relationship with
the economic elite, most of whom are urban dwellers. While some
landowners and merchants saw themselves as partners with their
farming clients, many owners and lenders saw farmers solely in
terms of profit regardless of the consequences to individual farmers
or society as a totality. Foreclosures and indebtedness that destroys
families is just an (un)intended consequence of the profit motive
and reflect good business practices that will benefit our families
and ensure the good life of the wealthy and those aspiring toward
upward economic mobility.

The Book of Amos describes the opulence of urban dwellers
who have country estates, financed by the exploitation of peasants.
Their largesse is bought at the price of the poverty of peasants, some
of whom must sell themselves into bondage to pay off their debts.[28]

Eighth century BCE Israel is not alone in using predatory
lending practices for material gain. In the United States, such
usurious lending was a major cause of the mortgage crisis of 2007-
2010, in which high-risk mortgage applicants were persuaded by
lenders to purchase homes at subprime interest rates only to have
the rates increase or balloon beyond the borrower's ability to pay,
leading to approximately 1,000,000 foreclosures and economic
recession by October 2008. While millions of persons lost their
homes, mortgage lenders and banks, considered too big to fail,
were bailed out by the government. The bail outs of banks and
investment houses may have been necessary to prevent immediate
economic collapse, but tragically those who received the predatory
loans, often under false pretenses, had only modest redress and
found their lives in shambles. To these American predatory lenders,
the goal was making money, regardless of its impact on the home
buyer and their family.

Amos asserts that there is ultimately a cost to economic injustice that far outweighs the benefits to the leisure and privileged

---

28 For a description of rent capitalism in general and as related to Amos,
see Bernhard Lang, *Monotheism and the Prophetic Minority* (Sheffield,
England: The Almond Press, 1983), 116-126.

class. If the wealthy and powerful turn away from God's vison of Shalom, they will not only experience a famine of hearing the word of God (8:11-13), eventually their nation will collapse, and they will lose their national sovereignty and personal security. Amos experiences national catastrophe in terms of divine punishment. God is the ultimate force in history and human life and those who stands in God's way will be decimated.

Many people today recognize the reality of divine judgment but balance their understanding of judgment with a divine gracefulness that Amos might not have envisioned. In contrast to Amos, progressive Christians, influenced by process-relational theology, see military and national catastrophes as the result of human decision-making not the hand of God. We believe that what humans do in terms of economic and ecological stewardship contributes to forest fires, floods, and hurricanes, environmental collapse, injustice and oppression may eventuate in political chaos. The interplay of civil war and famine, along with ineffective and despotic leadership, leads to refugees leaving their homelands in search of freedom and survival. Human agency can both cure and kill. We don't need to attribute plague and pestilence to divine retribution. God seeks wholeness for all people, most especially the vulnerable, and defying God's moral arc will eventually lead to national and planetary catastrophe.

I believe that while God is involved in historical processes and natural events, in contrast to Amos, I hold that God is not the ultimate perpetrator of destruction. God works toward national and personal healing, but God's moral arc is thwarted by human decision-making. Our choices shape the impact of God's presence in the world, adding to or limiting God's influence on the world. Philosopher Alfred North Whitehead spoke of God's action in the world in terms of ideals and relevant possibilities, emerging in the interplay of divine inspiration and human decision-making. Openness to God's vision increases of creativity and aligns us with the God-inspired moral arc of history. According to Whitehead, the initial aim, God's vision in the micro and macro, may be understood as "analogous to the remorseless working of things in Greek and in Buddhist thought. The initial aim is the best for that impasse. But if the best be bad, then the ruthlessness of God can be personified as Ate, the goddess of mischief. The chaff is burnt."[29] Sometimes the best that God can do – especially in the context of human destructiveness, whether intentional or the result of apathy – is to minimize the destruction that must occur due to the relationship of actions to consequences. God works with the world as it is in all its tragedy and beauty, steering the moral and spiritual arcs of history through the wilderness and chaos of human choice. Divine transformation, challenging our nation's status quo, may seem painful, especially if we must sacrifice present privilege for the greater good. But the goal is always healing – the healing of our souls and the soul of the nation. God feels the pain of poor and rich alike when lives and nations collapse.

In whatever ways we understand God's work in the world, clearly, Amos sees chaos and misery as the consequence of turning away from God's vision of justice and hospitality. The prophet predicts that the Northern and Southern Kingdoms alike will experience devastation that will terrify even the most courageous among us. There will be nowhere to run and nowhere to hide. Wealth and military power will not be able to save us from the impact of our actions as the planet itself cries out against us.

Harsh words come from the Holy One. What the Northern Kingdom could not imagine occurring to them as God's chosen will become an inevitability unless they pause, notice, confess, and turn to God's path of justice. In the wake of the "impossibility" of pandemic and near economic collapse in our time, Amos' words shatter the complacency of all who are willing to listen, then and now.

> So, I will press you down in your place,
>   just as a cart presses down
>   when it is full of sheaves.

---

29 Alfred North Whitehead, *Process and Reality: Corrected Edition* (New York: Free Press, 1978), 244.

Flight shall perish from the swift,
   and the strong shall not retain their strength,
   nor shall the mighty save their lives;
those who handle the bow shall not stand,
   and those who are swift of foot shall not save themselves,
   nor shall those who ride horses save their lives;
and those who are stout of heart among the mighty
   shall flee away naked in that day,
says the LORD. (4:13-16)

The questions that Amos leaves for the Northern Kingdom and for us remain unanswered: Will we listen to God's voice or drown it out as we cling to our way of life? Will we open our senses to God's voice in the pain of the human and non-human world? Is it too late for us to change our ways?

Is The United States That Exceptional? The myth of American exceptionalism emerges in some of the most interesting places. At a recent school board meeting in Ottawa Country, Michigan, in which persons, who presumed themselves to be good patriotic Christians, protested mask mandates and other COVID precautions, the following was reported:

> At least one man, his voice dripping with sarcasm, called the commissioners "petty tyrants" and promoted a group formed to press elected officials into signing pledges that recognize the "nation's Judeo-Christian heritage and celebrate America as an exceptional nation blessed by God. We stand united to restore and amplify the principles of American exceptionalism."[30]

Many Americans believe that the United States alone fulfills God's vision for humankind. In their estimation, no other nation has the moral and altruistic vision of the United States. They believe no other nation has sacrificed as much as the United States to make the world a better place, many believe. Our competitors and opponents are immoral while we are altruistic, generous, and fair. We are truly exceptional in might and morality, they assert,

---

30 https://whtc.com/2021/08/25/ottawa-co-commission/

while denying a history of slavery, genocide, misogyny, intervention in other countries, and attacks on democracy such as the domestic terrorism of January 6, 2021, enacted by political leaders and their minions. While it is important that we affirm the "O beautiful for spacious skies," "pilgrim feet," and "heroes proved," we need to remember that "God shed his (sic.) grace" on every land and that our history, like that of every other country, is ambiguous, filled with moments of generosity and heroism as well as villainy and violence.

Perhaps no modern leader captured the spirit of American exceptionalism than Ronald Reagan. In his "city on a hill" speech, Reagan waxed poetic in his spiritual affirmation of America's unique moral status among nations:

> You can call it mysticism if you want to, but I have always believed that there was some divine plan that placed this great continent between two oceans to be sought out by those who were possessed of an abiding love of freedom and a special kind of courage.

Reagan was not the first to proclaim that America, both before and after the American Revolution, is an exceptional land. From the very beginning, European settlers saw their "errand in the wilderness" as the result of divine providence. Long before Reagan's speech, in 1630 John Winthrop proclaimed the American experiment as a "city on a hill." Like the children of Israel's pilgrimage to the promised land, European settlers believed that they were destined to settle this land between two oceans, securing religious and economic freedom, regardless of the consequences to its indigenous peoples or to those who they kidnapped from their homelands, impressing them into slavery. In contrast to today's unrestrained capitalists, it must be mentioned that Winthrop believed God required integrity and fairness of God's chosen people. In the spirit of the Israelites' conquest of Canaan, European settlers believed that they had a divinely chosen manifest destiny to occupy and civilize this land. They saw themselves as the New Israel, God's chosen, bringing God to the heathen. Whatever they "discovered" was theirs even if it was already inhabited by the continent's First People. Later as the United States found itself in a Civil War, and just a month before announcing the Emancipation Proclamation, Abraham Lincoln proclaimed America's vocation, hoping that we would once again be united:

> We shall nobly save, or meanly lose, the last best hope of earth. Other means may succeed; this could not fail. The way is plain, peaceful, generous, just — a way which, if followed, the world will forever applaud, and God must forever bless.

God's providence has made us superior to our neighbors, indeed the "last best hope of earth." In our estimation, we surely aren't like China, Russia, North Korea, Cuba, or Venezuela. We claim, often with good reason, that their "socialism" damages the human spirit in contrast to our soul-uplifting free market capitalism and individualistic initiative. The "old world" of Europe, we think, is good but it lacks the drive and initiative – the innovation – of our land. We tout that we are the planet's oldest democracy and unlike other lands, in America, every social and economic barrier can be shattered and any "boy" (sic.) can grow up to be president.

Motivated by their belief in divine providence, European Americans sojourned across the land, doing what their faith affirmed as the necessary but dirty work of displacing and decimating its indigenous peoples, profiting from slavery, to take the stage as a political and military power, the last great hope for democracy. Of course, like the Israelites, American history is ambiguous, as I noted earlier. We have done great things as a nation and have rebuilt the lands of former enemies and we have sought to make the world safe for democracy, but we have also undermined democracies to promote our interests, entered unnecessary wars, exploited other nations for their resources, and placed profits over human and planetary wellbeing. To the children of slaves and indigenous peoples, the words of Langston Hughes still ring true, "America never was America to me."

Yet is America truly exceptional, unparalleled, or first among equals? Does our unique history separate us from all other nations? And can we be patriotic and affirm the significance of other nations and the reality that the people of other nations love their country as much as we love our own?

The details are obvious to a student of history or current observer that the United States is a fallible and imperfect country. Our infrastructure is crumbling. Nearly 140 million persons struggle to make ends meet. A home repair, car repair, or health crisis can put millions of families in financial peril. Millions belong to the working poor, going to work each day and having little to show for it beyond paying the rent and buying groceries. In the pandemic, the wealthiest 1% flourished while many "essential workers" – home health aides, food packers, farm workers, maintenance persons – struggled to feed their families and succumbed to the Covid virus. And sadly, the once touted American democracy is in jeopardy, not only in terms of the failed insurrection of January 6, 2021, but mistrust of election results, gerrymandering and voting restrictions, and the rise of white Christian nationalism and vigilante justice. Class, race, and economics still determine the fate of tens of millions for whom the American Dream more closely resembles a nightmare. Though 2800 years have passed, the words of Amos condemn our nation's misplaced values, consumerism, and policies that advantage the wealthy to the detriment of the economically vulnerable.

No doubt Amos was told to go back home or, now that he was in the Northern Kingdom, to silence his voice. "Israel, love it or leave it," the elite jeered. The same stridency seeks to drown out the message of those who challenge the foundations of American exceptionalism and free market capitalism or who dare remind us of our history of slavery, destruction of indigenous peoples, and ongoing racism in politics, economics, and the justice system, whether in the political arena, social media, or school boards. To challenge these national golden calves leads to the accusation of hating America and promoting the evil of socialism. Prophets are

seldom welcomed in their own or any other land! Lock them up!
Send them packing! They don't belong in the land of the free and
the home of the brave!

In a time in which patriotism is often identified in the United
States with questioning election results, protecting white privilege,
supporting authoritarianism and drowning out dissent, and seeking to return to the values of the 1950s if not earlier, when people
"knew their place," our survival as a nation requires a more spacious
and humble patriotism. We cannot move forward without confessing the ambiguities and injustices of our history. Transformation
comes through embracing the totality of our history and not just
the idealized past. We must confess our national sins, lament the
pain we have caused, and work to restore the damage done by
slavery and genocide. Then we will embody a patriotism grounded
not only in love for our country but love of the planet, the patriotic
vision described in "This is My Song":

> This is my song, Oh God of all the nations,
> A song of peace for lands afar and mine.
> This is my home, the country where my heart is;
> Here are my hopes, my dreams, my sacred shrine.
> But other hearts in other lands are beating,
> With hopes and dreams as true and high as mine.
> My country's skies are bluer than the ocean,
> And sunlight beams on cloverleaf and pine.
> But other lands have sunlight too and clover,
> And skies are everywhere as blue as mine.
> Oh hear my song, oh God of all the nations,
> A song of peace for their land and for mine.[31]

In confessing our tragic and heroic history and recognizing the
distance that remains between our current national situation and
the dream of a "more perfect union," our newfound humility will
enable us to be a positive force in healing the earth and speaking for
justice everywhere. Living out the dream of a truly moral nation, we
will "crown our good with [personhood] from sea to shining sea."

---

31   Also known as "A Song of Peace," taken from a poem by Lloyd Stone.

LISTENING TO THE PROPHET AMOS

Confession is an essential aspect of personal, institutional, and national healing. The point of confession is not paralyzing guilt or denial of positive achievements, but a recognition of our whole personal and national history, in both their highest and most destructive manifestations. Confession is the prelude to transformation and entering a process of recovery, restoration, and reparation.

Spiritual practice. Prayerfully consider our national history. For what are you thankful? Reflect on the blessings of our land.

Again, ponder our nation's past and present history. For what do we need to repent? Reflect on moments of injustice and devastation in our nation's history. Prayerfully consider how you can, in your setting, be an agent of national healing.

QUESTIONS FOR REFLECTION

1) Have you ever had the experience of "schadenfreude," delight at another's misfortune? What behaviors provoked this experience?

2) How do you understand God and God's relationship to humankind? What is God's role in pain and suffering? Is God beyond history or does God truly experience the cries of the poor? Does God respond to our personal suffering or the suffering caused by institutional decision-making?

3) How would you describe Amos' understanding of divine punishment? Does God directly punish us for injustice or unethical behavior?

4) Are there other ways to understand the relationships of acts and consequences than seeing destruction as the direct result of divine activity?

5) How has your understanding of American history changed over the years? What stories did you hear as a child? What other histories have you heard that challenge these stories?

6) Why is it important to hear stories of racial and economic injustice, even when they challenge your previous assumptions? What are the reasons people resist hearing about the historical reality and impact of economic and racial privilege?

7) From Amos' perspective, does America need to be concerned about divine judgment? Are we truly exceptional and thus protected from the consequences of our injustice?

Prayer. Loving God, help me see the relationships between acts and consequences and the impact of injustice on our nation and the world. Help me to listen to the cries of the poor. Inspire me to find ways to restore and repair the damage our nation has caused to our people and the planet. Let me be an agent in healing the soul of our nation and the planet. Amen.

CHAPTER SIX

WAKE UP TO THE
SIGNS OF THE TIMES

(Amos, Chapters 3 and 4)

I sent among you a pestilence
after the manner of Egypt ...
And you did not return to me. (4:10)

If you want comfort from the Bible, initially you won't find it in the Book of Amos. Amos, at first glance, has little compassion for the affluent communities and religious and governmental officials of Judah and Israel. To the prophet, the anxieties of the elite and powerful pale in comparison to the pain they have inflicted, albeit unintentionally in many cases, on their landless, vulnerable, and impoverished kin. No doubt, many of the affluent know exactly what they are doing and justify the pain they cause as collateral damage in their quest for economic and military security. Others are simply unable to connect the dots between their wealth and others' poverty and are good-hearted, but oblivious to the pain they cause for others. Contributions to the food bank and donations to the temple suffice to ease their conscience. They don't know, but will they care when Amos lays out the cost of their culpability?

Amos is not a fortune teller or soothsayer. He simply knows, in the spirit of Marvin Gaye's song, "What's goin' on?" The pain and anguish of the dispossessed are writ large for those with eyes to see, or as another song of the 1960s alerts, "the words of the prophets are written on the subway walls and tenement halls." But, will we see, and if we do see, will we respond and choose to become God's partners in repairing and restoring the world, sacrificing our comfort, and transforming our institutions to reflect God's vision of Shalom? Will the "sounds of silence" shock us into hearing so that we may take the trouble to discern "What's goin' on?" Will members of the wealthy and powerful, be touched by God's vision of Shalom and judgment, choose against their own best interests and the interests of their economic class, to make the good trouble necessary to bring justice and healing to the land?

Amos is appalled by his kinfolk's inability to discern the signs of the times. They delight in their prosperity and cry "peace, peace, when there is no peace." (Jeremiah 8:11) The house is on fire, and they carry on as if nothing is happening, life is going on as usual, and they amass profits at the expense of the wellbeing of future generations.

Chapters 1 to 4 of Amos have been described as the "Book of Doom" and Amos' message in these chapters is relevant to America and every nation today. Consider recent reports from the Departments of Defense and Homeland Security and the National Security Council that chart the relationship between climate change and national security. According to these reports, if not halted, climate change will lead to: "Worsening conflict within and between nations. Increased dislocation and migration as people flee climate-filled instability. Heightened military tension and uncertainty. Financial hazards." Not to mention putting the lives of our children and grandchildren at risk.[32] Changes in weather patterns are currently wreaking havoc, just as Covid did, first and most devastatingly on the poor of the developing nations and the United States, and eventually transform the lives of the wealthy and powerful. Borders will be overrun by refugees and asylum seekers. Supply chains will collapse, and prices skyrocket due to the impact of climate change.

The military, corporate, and political establishment know "what's goin' on?" but will we as a nation have the will to respond? Will we sacrifice for the present and future well-being of our kin?

---

32   Christopher Flavell, Julien E. Barnes, Eileen Sullivan, Jennifer Steinhauer, "Reports Lay Out Climate's Change to U.S. Security," *New York Times* (Friday, October 22, 1, 13).

That is Amos' question to us. The signs of the times are clear, the house is on fire, with catastrophic forest fires throughout the West. We are being swamped, with record floods and hurricanes in the Southeast and Caribbean.

Amos' words to the Northern Kingdom are harsh. He sounds heartless in his words of doom. Yet, I believe that his prophetic anger is motivated by love. He could have said "no" to God and enjoyed his comfortable life in Tekoa. But he risks reputation, wellbeing, and personal happiness, and leaves his family, to share God's message, hoping that somehow his Northern kin will repent, change their ways, and escape the catastrophes on the horizon. Amos speaks as a fellow countryman to his kin. His heart is breaking at the threats he perceives. He feels the pain of the vulnerable as well as the pain that will eventually come to the wealthy and powerful and their innocent children if the nation's leaders refuse to respond to the signs of the times. This is tough love, but Amos' urgency is born out of a sense of empathetic connection and dread at the suffering on the horizon if we fail to listen to God's message. Perhaps, if its northern neighbors repent, the Southern Kingdom, Amos' homeland, will also change its ways.

You are My Own! (Amos 3:1-2) One thing you can say about Amos is that he leaves no doubt about where God and he stand in relation to injustice. Amos repeats the same judgment in a variety of ways to emphasize how important the people's response is to their survival. Accordingly, I will abbreviate many of Amos' threats in the chapters to come. My precis of Amos' vision of divine judgment in no way minimizes the importance of his words to the Northern Kingdom and us.

According to God's indictment of Israel, Israel is exceptional in its relationship to God, although it is also unexceptional in its ethical behavior. God has called this people out of nothingness, delivered them from captivity, and given them a promised land. The children of Israel have a vocation – to live out God's love in a holy way, to be a model of God's vision of what the world can be like, just and compassionate in personal and political relationships.

No doubt other nations and people have vocations, but this moral and religious vision is at the heart of Israel's identity.

I am not sure if I like – or approve of – Amos' understanding of divine intimacy. Perhaps, the prophet is proclaiming a precursor to Jesus' words to another wayward community eight centuries later, "From everyone to whom much has been given, much will be required; and from the one to whom much has been entrusted, even more will be demanded." (Luke 12:48) The oracle's message seems like overkill. "I will punish you for all your iniquities." (3:2) There appears to be no mercy, grace, or forgiveness. No "Father, forgive them for they know not what they are doing" in God's response to Israel's misdeeds. Troubled by Amos' vision of coercive and unilateral divine power, I would revise Amos' oracle to read, "You will suffer the results of your injustice. The choice is yours. I have given you a vision of the future. If you fail to act, there is nothing I can do to prevent this, and despite your disobedience, I will feel your pain." I have the same difficulty in reading Hosea's misogynist treatment of the wayward Gomer as symbolic of God's relationship with wayward Israel.

Acts and Consequences. (Amos 3:3-8) Amos is the prophet of interdependence. Everything is interconnected. We are all, as Martin Luther King noted, part of an intricate and dynamic fabric of relatedness in which our well-being is connected to the well-being of others. Amos would understand the "butterfly effect," the recognition that a butterfly flapping its wings in California can be a factor in weather changes on the Eastern seaboard. As Francis Thompson avers:

> All things by immortal power
> Near or far
> Hiddenly
> To each other linked are
> That thou canst not stir a flower
> Without troubling a star.

For Amos, the most pitiable person, group, or nation is the one whose values constellate around independence and individualism, and who does not know their dependence on others and the impact of their deeds on the wellbeing of the community. We are all in the same storm and Amos reminds us that we need to see and then act as if we are in the same boat, sinking or swimming together.

Amos speaks of lions roaring, birds being ensnared, trumpets blaring, cities being destroyed, and friends meeting for a walk as examples of cause and effect. When you see one thing, you can assume that it is connected to another. Nothing is isolated. For those with eyes to see, the appearance of one thing – poverty, violence, incivility – is connected to other things, for example, greed and injustice, alienation, and political prevarication and incitement.

Again, I struggle with Amos' vision of divine activity, and while I cannot soften his words, I must suggest an alternative to the prophet's question, "Does disaster befall a city, unless the Lord has done it?" (3:6) Amos no doubt viewed God as directly acting in the world to reward and punish. To the prophet, everything flowed from God's hand, both good and ill. In contrast, while not blunting the consequences of injustice, I assert that in an interdependent universe, within the dynamic fabric of relationships, violations of the moral arc have consequences and they can be devasting. These connections reflect the divine order of cause and effect, built into a predictable reality, one we depend on for our daily lives, but not God's direct choice or action. I recall a pastor whose wisdom I respect telling me of an encounter with a congregant dying of lung cancer, who noted, "I'm not angry at God for the cancer. I smoked for forty years. This was my doing, not God's." The same can be said for the consequences of consumerism, racism, greed, and lack of a common national vision. If not addressed, they will eventually lead to civil unrest, environmental destruction, and the unraveling of the social order. Creativity and freedom are essential in human life. Our decisions can shape the world around us. The impact of our choices is not random. There is an order, a moral arc, that when transgressed can lead to chaos and disorder. The consequences of injustice can be altered by changing our behaviors and public policy, but the consequences of injustice are real, first, for the vulnerable, and then for the perpetrator. We can wake up to climate change, respond with urgency, and minimize the catastrophes that lie ahead! If we do nothing, our nation and our children and grandchildren will experience global catastrophe.

Amos concludes this section with a word – perhaps autobiographical – about the prophetic vocation.

> Surely the Lord GOD does nothing, without revealing his secret to his servants the prophets. The lion has roared; who will not fear? The Lord GOD has spoken; who can but prophesy? (v. 7-8)

The signs of the times are not hidden. They are there for all to see, revealed in natural disaster, political upheaval, and prophetic word. But only a handful of observers truly glimpse the deeper messages of political, meteorological, and cultural shifts. These perceptive spirits must speak when they hear God whispering within current events. They can no longer sit on the sidelines, assuming they can escape the dangers that lie ahead. Inspired, perhaps, even compelled, by their vision, they must share, out of love and empathy, and concern for future generations, what may occur unless the nation changes its ways.

Get On the Right Path. (3:9-15) The religious, political, and economic elite have lost their spiritual and ethical GPS. "They don't know how to do right." (3:10) Their attempts to "fix" things only exacerbate the problems. Like many today, they want justice without change or sacrifice. They may regret the growing gap between the rich and the poor, but they don't want to make the sacrifices that will lead to greater well-being for the vulnerable. While we can't make a one-to-one correspondence with the economics of the Northern Kingdom and our current economic or tax system, few of the American privileged want to pay a higher percentage of their income in taxes, pay higher wages or benefits to their workers, or make reparations for past injustices. Everyday people are challenged to pay higher fuel prices to be in solidarity with the people of Ukraine or respond to climate change, paying the true cost of fossil fuel use, and many "patriotic" Americans are upset! Personal generosity, arbitrary, optional, and individualistic, won't uplift the poor when the system itself works against their wellbeing.

No doubt the privileged remembered the "mythical" statutes related to the Jubilee (Leviticus 25:1-3), Sabbatical years (Exodus 21:2; 23:10-11), intended to repair economic equalities due to the decisions of previous generations or the loss of property due to accident or chance, and the principle of leaving the wheat the farm workers missed to be gleaned by the economically vulnerable (Leviticus 19:9-10). Such measures were no doubt seen as idealistic but impractical in the real world of the Northern Kingdom. Many of the privileged, then and now, may have subscribed to viewpoints such as: God helps those who help themselves; poverty is the result of laziness; or people are poor because of prior bad decisions or moral failure. God has, after all, blessed the privilege with their largesse. Their lifestyles and affluence - and summer and winter homes - don't need justification, while the poor need to account for every benefit they receive. In our time, politicians speak of "welfare queens" or harshly judge persons on state assistance for spending money on cable television, alcohol, or entertainment, while they enjoy technologies and travel to places that economically disadvantaged families can only dream about.

When the powerful lose their spiritual GPS, religious, economic, and national wellbeing is endangered. The religious centers at Gilgal and Bethel will be leveled along with the summer and winter homes of the wealthy. Faith without works of mercy and sacrifice – religious practices that justify opulence while accepting poverty as normal – destroys the credibility and witness of religious institutions. In the wake of the Covid pandemic, a megachurch, whose prosperity gospel pastor's net worth is valued at $50 million has recently returned over $4 million in Payment Protection

Program loans. It is more than bad optics when billion-dollar corporations pay virtually no taxes and megachurches garner millions from government programs, while small businesses close and the working poor are evicted. When I recall a poster from the sixties that asked, "If you were accused of being a follower of Jesus, would there be enough evidence to convict you?" I am forced to look at my own lifestyle and the advantages I take for granted while others lose their homes, receive food baskets, or must flee their countries due to climate change or political instability.

Cows of Bashan and Superficial Spirituality. (4:1-8) I must admit that I am a pastor, professor, and spiritual guide rather than a prophet. I go at things slant and not directly like Amos. My critiques are gentle. I don't hurl ethical and spiritual hand grenades like Amos. Yet, there is a time for prophetic anger and righteous indignation to shock the "haves" from apathy to empathy, and from consumerism to sacrificial living. As Howard Thurman proclaims, the oppressor must be confronted with their injustice not just for the sake of the homeless and marginalized, those who are politically and economically dispossessed by a stroke of a pen or a legislative vote, but to save the oppressors' own souls.

There is little tenderness and perhaps some intended misogyny, inappropriate in today's world, in Amos' diatribe against the "cows of Bashan." Amos is equal opportunity in his denunciation of injustice. While there is little doubt that the Northern Kingdom was patriarchal, Amos asserts that elite urban wives were complicit in their husband's unjust business dealings. They also "oppress the poor" and "crush the needy," asking their husbands to "bring them something to drink," to satisfy their desires for comfort.

Even their attitude toward religious institutions indicts them of injustice. "You love to make showy offerings," Amos jeers. "You endow buildings, support good music, publish your gifts in the church register, but a widow's mite resounds more favorably in God's eyes than apparent generosity supported by unjust business practices." Amos believes that before you contribute to the brick, mortar, and music of the worship centers, you must care for the vulnerable and practice virtue in the marketplace. Generosity must be institutional and systemic as well as individual. Religious traditions falter when they become bastions of the status quo or serve the interests of the wealthy and powerful whether in ancient Israel, contemporary oligarchic Russia and authoritarian China, and economically unjust El Salvador or the United States.

Consider the transformation of Oscar Romero (1917-1980) from privileged priest and friend of the rich and famous to activist and prophet. When Romero was appointed Archbishop of El Salvador, the politically active members of the priesthood were disappointed, sure that he would turn a deaf ear to the cries of the poor. In contrast, the wealthy applauded the decision, believing that we would be an apostle of the status quo, supporting their interests looking the other way, if they contributed to the coffers of the church. Both groups expected that Romero would maintain business as usual, heavenly-minded and no earthy good, in terms of the church's involvement in political and economic change. Both activists and wealthy landowners were amazed when, following the murder of a dear friend at the hands of the oligarchs, the scales fell from Romero's eyes, awakening him to God's presence in the cries of the poor and God's suffering in the pain of the disinherited. As the prophetic pastor of the people, who sought reconciliation through compassionate actions, Romero discovered that being a faithful pastor called him to support the interests of the poor and vulnerable over the wealthy and powerful. He knew that listening to God's voice required listening to the cries of the poor and advocating for social transformation. The wealthy saw him as a traitor and sought to strip him of his episcopal status. He lived with death threats. Eventually, he was shot while celebrating the mass.

The examples of Oscar Romero, Martin Luther King, and Dorothy Day remind us that when a religious leader promotes individual spiritual growth and congratulates the wealthy on their generosity, they are described as pious. When they counsel social change, they are seen as the enemy of the state and often martyred for preaching the word of the prophets and Jesus.[33]

God is Still Speaking. Is Anybody Listening? (4:9-11)   Amos has a profound sense of God's nearness. The God for whom he speaks does not have a human voice and thus needs prophets to be divine messengers. The message they are challenged to share to their kin emerges from God's experience of the world's sorrow and joy. God is the Ultimate Empath. The Most Moved Mover and Heart of the Universe. God feels our pain and needs us to be God's hands and hearts and feet. Spanish Mystic Teresa of Avila (1515-1582) reminds us:

> Christ has no body now but yours.
> No hands, no feet on earth but yours.
> Yours are the eyes through which he looks compassion on this world.
> Yours are the feet with which he walks to do good.
> Yours are the hands through which he blesses all the world.
> Yours are the hands, yours are the feet, yours are the eyes, you are his body.
> Christ has no body now on earth but yours.

Because God feels, Amos must speak. But will they listen? Will we listen to the prophets of our time?

The God of the Universe demands our attention. The symptoms of injustice are registered in changing weather patterns, potentially threatening the nation's economy and national security, and felt first by the poor, who cannot escape what Amos believes is God's megaphone to humanity through:

✓   Famine and the attending malnourishment and starvation.
✓   Drought and crop damage.

---

33 For more on the interplay of mysticism and social transformation, including the spirituality of Oscar Romero, see Bruce Epperly, *Mystics in Action: Twelve Saints for Today* (Maryknoll, NY: Orbis Press, 2020).

✓ Unstable weather conditions, flooding rains in one town; drought, and water shortage in another.
✓ Blight and mildew that destroy crops.
✓ Pestilence/pandemic killing humans and non-humans alike, carrying away even the fittest.
✓ Natural catastrophes, like those which destroyed Sodom and Gomorrah.

Despite these signs of the times, manifestations of divine displeasure, Amos proclaims in words resembling a liturgical litany, the divine oracles four times, "yet you did not return to me." Frustrated with their injustice and apathy God asks, "What will it take for these people to realize the precarious nature of their current situation? What will it take for them to realize that their injustice is the cause of climatological, agricultural, and seismic disasters?" And we wonder, "What will it take for us to realize that our environmental injustice – after all, the poor are at greatest risk from catastrophic climate changes, famine, flood, and pandemic – is responsible for severe weather events?" The signs of the times are written in weather patterns and social upheaval, but will we mend our ways?

While God did not send AIDS and or the Hurricane Katrina to condemn America's acceptance of homosexuality, as some preachers have suggested, I believe that in the orderly movements of nature and humankind, going against the moral and spiritual arcs of justice and human wellbeing has consequences. Putting self-interest above public welfare eventually has dire results for rich and poor alike. These words echo to contemporary America. A USA president pulls out of an international climate accord on a whim, knowing the consequences of his actions. Congress blocks meaningful climate change legislation. States continue to promote fossil fuels rather than renewable sources of energy. Attacks on the Capitol are viewed as tourist trips and voting rights for minorities are restricted as they were in the Jim Crow era. In this "Christian nation," profits outweigh the words of prophets resounding through changes in weather patterns, melting ice caps, and species extinction. And yet "they will not return to me!"

The Glory of God and Human Destiny. (4:12-13) The Book of Doom concludes with both an invitation or is it a threat and a theophany. Prepare to meet your God. Given the prelude, this is not necessarily good news. God cannot be fully found in designated holy places. God cannot be confined by our religious and political systems. At best, they point to the Holy One. Our religious systems, our elaborate worship, and our monetary endowments stand in the way of authentic relationship with the Holy One if we do not find God in the poor and forgotten. Meeting God means facing our injustice and apathy, and our complicity in injustice. As prosperous citizens, with "stock" portfolios (either found in our pastures or Wall Street), our comfort – and even our generosity – may indirectly crush the vulnerable and impoverished. We must face our institutional sinfulness, recognize the consequences for us and the poor, and then choose to listen or deny God's guidance.

In the spirit of Psalm 8 or Job 38-41, we are confronted by the juxtaposition of the Infinite and intimate, the Cosmic and the finite. The God of Hosts forms the mountains, creates the winds, reveals truth to mystics and prophets, and moves through all creation, heaven and earth alike. God is not to be trifled with. God is majestic and mysterious, and powerful and personal. Beyond our imagination and yet caring for each of us. God is righteous and just and stands against anything that defaces God's glory embodied in human life. The second century CE church theologian Irenaeus (130-202) proclaimed that the glory of God is a fully alive human. We are all intended to live abundantly and fully, to achieve the vocations toward which God is calling us. Yet, the human vocation of full humanity is stunted by poverty and disenfranchisement. Dreams are dashed and possibilities amputated. Apathy, consumerism, greed, and political and economic manipulation also stunt the souls of the wealthy and powerful. The powerful lose their ability to empathize and feel, and live by fear of change, rather than love their kinfolk. Still, Amos speaks of a glorious God who wants both powerful and poor to be healed. This can only happen through the repentance that shapes personal and corporate morality.

LISTENING TO THE PROPHET AMOS

Ubuntu! I am because of you. We are because of one another. This is the intricate fabric of relatedness that joins all of us, human and non-human, the world of cities and the world of nature. Our hope is in moving from self-interest to world loyalty, loving our nation, and seeking the well-being of all its people to, more importantly, loving the good earth, the "body of God," from whom all blessings flow.

Spiritual Practice. Begin with a time of silence, breathing in and out your connection with the universe and your human kin. Take time to reread Amos 4:12-13 along with Psalm 8. What images of God and humankind come to mind? Where do you experience God's glory? In light of Irenaeus' vision of the glory of God as a fully alive human, where do you experience God's glory? What stands in the way of you experiencing God's glory? What social practices stand in the way of others experiencing God's glory? Toward what does this experience call you?

QUESTIONS FOR REFLECTION

1) Listen to Marvin Gaye's "What's Goin' On." What issues does the singer-songwriter notice as dangers to human wellbeing? Are these issues still current in American society?

2) How do you judge our nation's responsibility to respond to climate change in light of the Department of Defense and Homeland Security and National Security Council reports on global climate change? What should we do, governmentally, institutionally, and personally?

3) In what ways is Amos' anger at the economic and political policies of Israel related to his love for his people? Is it possible to balance righteous indignation with love of nation?

4) How does Amos understand Israel's chosen status? Does the United States have a particular vocation? Are we judged like Israel in terms of our vocation?

5) Where has our nation deviated from the "right way?" How might we right our nation?

6) What are the "signs of the times" that you notice? Are we responding to them? What might we do in response?

7) Do you think God – or the planet – speaks to us in catastrophes? Is there a sense of cause and effect to which we need to pay attention?

8) How do understand the relationship between God's glory and human wellbeing? How do we respond to practices that stand in the way of persons experiencing God's glory?

Prayer. Break my heart, Heart of All Things, that I may feel the pain of poverty and violence. Open my senses that I may experience the connection between my privilege and others' powerlessness. Deliver me from hopelessness of change that I might in my time and place choose my vocation as God's companion in healing the earth and its peoples. Amen.

Chapter Seven

Justice Like An Everflowing Stream

(Amos, Chapters 5 and 6)

But let justice roll down like waters,
and righteousness
like an ever-flowing stream.
(Amos 5:24)

Is the Northern Kingdom's fate sealed? Is there any hope for a wayward nation in the immediate future or the long stretch of history? The answer appears to be, "That depends." In many ways, Amos' pronouncements are like the words that the legendary Jonah proclaimed to Nineveh, "Forty days and Nineveh shall be overthrown." (Jonah 3:4) In this multi-layered tale, the reluctant prophet, still drying off from his journey in the belly of a great fish, has no love for Nineveh, the home of the Assyrian conquerors of the Northern Kingdom four decades after Amos' call to repentance. In fact, Jonah would love to see God pulverize Nineveh and its people. To the prophet's chagrin, the community repents, goes on a fast and turns from its evil ways. "Who knows? God may relent and change the divine mind; God may turn from God's fierce anger so that we do not perish." (Jonah 3:9) And the great "perhaps" comes to pass.

> When God saw what they did, how they turned from their evil ways, God changed the divine mind about the calamity God said would be brought upon them; and God did not do it." (Jonah 3:10)

Amos, Chapters 5 and 6, suggests that deliverance is possible, but only if the people change their ways, and establish justice in law, economics, politics, and religion. We shape the future and the future we shape has an impact on God's presence in history and our lives.

Chapter 5 begins with a heartfelt call for social transformation, "Hear this word that I take up over you in lamentation, O house of Israel." (5:1) Unlike Jonah, Amos really cares. He sees the handwriting on the wall and is doing everything he can to give the people one last chance to repent. More importantly for the Northern Kingdom, God cares and is doing all that can be done to persuade them to change their ways.

God's passion is born out of pathos, empathy, and God's feeling the pain of the poor and the catastrophic suffering to come – to rich and poor alike – if the nation does not alter its ethical and spiritual course. Justice will roll down like waters, but will this ever-flowing stream destroy or nurture, flood or uplift? Ravage the complacent or heal the repentant? That is the great "perhaps."

Is the Future Settled? (5:1-17) Amos and many theologians throughout Christian history have considered the idea that God has decided or knows everything in advance. To many theists, nothing ever surprises God. They believe that God knows exactly what will happen in the lives of persons and nations. The future is preordained in its entirety and there is nothing we can do about it. Whatever happens from tidal wave to cancer and social upheaval is God's will. Even our salvation or damnation is decided in eternity, and the unsaved are "damned if they do, and damned if they don't."

Less severe but equally predetermined in approach is the belief that God knows exactly what will happen in an eternal unchanging now. To God, there is nothing new under the sun. The Northern Kingdom's fate is already known by God, and though they may appear to have agency, the outcome is sealed in eternity. Such believers assert that a God for whom new things occur or who adjusts to historical or personal changes is less perfect than a changeless, all-knowing, and all-determining God. They cannot imagine God in any way influenced by human behavior. Nor can they imagine God ever changing course in God's determination of the small and large events of history.

While Amos is clear that God knows the likelihood of national catastrophe, the fact – the actuality of national catastrophe occurring - is not yet settled. Speaking for God, Amos sees the future – humankind's and God's – as connected with how we respond to the prophet's message. Humans are not pawns in a divine chess game nor characters acting out an already written script. Rather, humans, individually and corporately, can change their minds, amend their behaviors, and become agents of alternative futures. Listen to these calls for individual and national decision:

> Seek me and live. (5:4)
> Seek the Lord and live, or God will break out against you. (5:6)
> Seek God and not evil that you may live, and so the Lord, the God of hosts, will be with you. (5:14)
> Hate evil and love good and establish justice in the gate; it may be that the Lord, the God of hosts, will be gracious to the remnant of Joseph. (5:15)
> But let justice roll down like waters, and righteousness like an ever-flowing stream. (5:25)

Each one of these demands is a call to decision. The prophet cries out, "Hear what God is saying to you in nature and international affairs and respond accordingly. Mend your ways. Turn from deceit and injustice and deliverance is possible. The future is open, and your actions now will shape the future. You make a difference to God and to the vulnerable of the land. Your choices will shape God's future and the shape of God's action in history. Will you mute the voice of God, drowning out the divine call with your praise songs and parties, and pursue the path of national destruction? Or will you listen to God's appeal, feel the pain of the vulnerable, feel God's pain, mend your ways, and change the course of history?" These are God's questions to the people of Israel, and these are God's questions to America today!

The reluctant prophet Jonah is surprised to discover that God changed God's mind and spared Nineveh in response to their repentance. Amos believes that God's involvement in the future is open to change as well, depending on the people's response to God's call for social transformation.

The love of God can comfort, and God can also afflict, Amos believes, in relationship to our openness to divine wisdom and our neighbor's need. The God of the Universe, "the one who made the Pleiades and Orion, and turns darkness into morning, and darkens the day into night" cares about the intimate details of our lives, the pain of the suffering, the callousness of injustice, the struggle of repentance. The Infinite is also the Intimate. The God of Israel is the Most Moved, not the Unmoved, Mover! Creation and destruction emerge as much from our decisions as God's. What will we choose and how will God respond in the orderly cause and effect of historical events?

Worship that Heals and Transforms. (5:18-27) In the biblical tradition, there is no place for individualistic, private, and purely personal religion. Biblical faith is holistic, grounded in following God's vision of Shalom, and sharing in God's goal of the divine realm "on earth as it is in heaven." The Epistle of James, written nine centuries after Amos' oracles, reflects the essence of biblical spirituality, "faith by itself, if it has no works, is dead." (2:17) Individual salvation is morally and spiritually bankrupt without corresponding works of love in your relationships and that includes your role as a citizen. Biblical spirituality is holistic, including mind, body, and spirit. From the exodus to the prophets, biblical spirituality also includes politics and economics. Written in a time in which the church had virtually no political power, and was, in fact, the object of political oppression, the Epistle of James castigates those who do not reach out to the vulnerable members of the community. Today, when churches and their leaders have potentially significant influence in politics and economics, James would be at the forefront of economic justice and social welfare programs. James seeks justice and that means equality in the law courts and in economic opportunity. Acts of the Apostles describes a community where the members share everything in common and addresses issues of inequity in the early Christian community.

(Acts 2:42-47; 3: 33-37) Today, in the United States where Christians are leaders in governance and economics, the spiritual leaders described in Acts of the Apostles would urge the church to be, as Martin Luther King observed, a headlight and not a taillight in ensuring the economic wellbeing of every citizen, and across the globe, and would challenge the growing economic gap between workers and owners in the corporate world. What happens in the communal sharing of the church is a model for all economic interactions – enough for everyone and privileging the common good over individual profit-making. Amos and James would both denounce the reactionary self-interest and racism evident among today's Christian nationalists, reveling in their claim to have a direct pipeline to God's plan for America. They would also challenge progressives who talk about justice and social change but do nothing to bring it about.

Amos believes worship is important. He is not counseling absence from religious rituals when he says:

> Seek me, and live;
> but do not seek Bethel,
> and do not enter into Gilgal
> or cross over to Beersheba. (5:5)

Amos is speaking to the wealthy and powerful whose lifestyles are built upon the suffering of their fellow citizens. Amos singles out those who rebuke prophetic voices, prefer national myth to political fact, trample the poor, levy high fees and taxes on the economically disadvantaged, and perpetuate injustice in the judicial system through bribery and preventing the poor from receiving due process. (5:10-13)

In today's language, Amos is saying "Don't go to church or consider yourself righteous, even if you make large donations, unless you feed the hungry, promote voting rights, ensure access and equality in the legal system, suspend foreclosures, and increase wages and benefits. Follow the prophets and not your profits!"

Amos has a personal relationship with God but a personal relationship with God is mere narcissism unless the prophet follows God's way, traveling to the Northern Kingdom to share God's vision. Amos is a contemplative activist, whose spirituality joins prayer and protest, meditation and listening to national news, and simple living so others can simply live.

Imagine Amos' anger at Christians bowing in prayer circles and then storming the USA Capitol on January 6. Visualize the prophet's vitriol at churches leading the charge against mask mandates and vaccinations and holding super spreader services. Ponder Amos' response to flag waving, "America first" worship services, identifying morally dubious politicians as God's saviors of America. Visualize Amos' disappointment in those who claim to be politically progressive, who talk the talk – like me – and yet see our individual economic stability as more important than global climate change or feeding the hungry.

While we cannot claim to know the details of Amos' view on American tax policy, clearly the prophet singles out those in his time who levy taxes on grain produced by struggling farmers while luxuriating on ivory couches, going to parties, and feasting on the best cuts of meat. Amos would, I suspect, take issue with billionaires and corporations that pay taxes at a lower rate than the middle class or lower middle class, or pay no taxes at all! Endowing a chapel or university will not erase the damage brought about by unfair and manipulative business practices.

Putting God first for Amos means putting your neighbor's well-being on the same level as your own economic interests. For Amos, there is no cheap grace. You love God by loving your neighbor, and your love of God inspires personal and corporate generosity and the creation of judicial and economic systems that serve the most vulnerable members of society. To those who say that the social gospel and liberation theology run contrary to the Bible, it is important to remember that Amos' words are primarily addressed to political, religious, and economic leaders, that is, to 8th century BCE political and economic priorities and not merely to isolated individuals. Holistic spirituality, then and now, is profoundly social and political, for as your nations and institutions "do unto the least of these" you do unto God! Going beyond party affiliation, prophetic healing embraces and challenges every leader and politically active person to seek justice and sacrifice for the greater good.

Is Change Possible? Can the People be Saved? (Amos 5:1-3; 6:1-14) Amos 5 begins with a dirge, with divine and human lamentation. Fallen is the virgin, youthful, nation, never to rise again. Though these words may be evocative and challenging, punctuated by a trumpet of warning, they are not predictive, they present the picture of a blessed nation that has failed to live up to its potential as a light to the nations. The chosen people have chosen to follow the way of greed and consumption rather than the god of justice. They poison justice with wormwood, letting the dishonest wealthy go unscathed while the honest poor leave empty-handed. The same would be said to a nation born of the affirmation of liberty and justice for all, and the equality of all people, but has been an agent of slavery, economic injustice, violence and disenfranchisement to minorities, and aggression and imperialism in international relations.

Complacent and confident in their military and economics, the stability of being God's chosen ones, they can't imagine being overrun by a neighboring nation. Equally confident in having the greatest military in the world, a can-do attitude, and an economy second to none, we overlook the homeless in the streets, parents living from paycheck to paycheck, inadequate medical care, and violence against minorities and immigrants. Certain of our democratic tradition, we can't imagine political leaders seeking – and almost achieving – a coup, attempting to overturn our election. Even after the attempted coup, broadcast before the whole world, many political leaders act as if nothing happened, claiming it was just a "tourist visit" to the United States Capitol. Will our unwarranted complacency and confidence lead to the collapse of our nation? Is our much-touted light on a hill on the verge of being snuffed out because of our nation's turning away from justice, equity, truth, and compassion? Will we decline while other nations, like China, rise?

Whenever we get puffed up about our nation's unique relationship to God, we would do well to remember the words of Abraham Lincoln in a time of national chaos. When Lincoln was asked, "Is God on his side?", the President replied, "Sir, my concern is not whether God is on our side, my greatest concern is to be on God's side, for God is always right."

All the National Days of Prayer won't make any difference, all the prayers in public schools will be of no avail, and all the God and country diatribes will have no effect, but will only further alienate us from God's vision, without justice rolling down like waters and righteousness like an ever-flowing stream.

LISTENING TO THE PROPHET AMOS

Mindfulness is at the heart of the prophetic vision. We need to know who we are and Whose we are. We need to examine the relationship between our lifestyle and the poverty of others, and the impact of our economic and foreign policy on persons across the nation and the planet.

Spiritual Practice. The Examen is a traditional Christian spiritual practice in which you review a particular day or period of your life in terms of your relationship with God. Our examen for this session will focus on spirituality and economics, your own and your congregation's.

Begin with a time of silence, opening to God's loving and empowering presence, asking for God's guidance and inspiration to see you live fully and honestly.

Then in the stillness give thanks for the blessings you have received, personal, institutional, relational, national. Thank God for God's loving fidelity and care for you and your loved ones, and for loving this world in its diversity.

Reflect on your spiritual life and social activism. What is the quality of your relationship with God? How would you evaluate in relation to God's love for all creation your relationship with the powerless and vulnerable? Where might you need to make changes in your life to be more faithful as a citizen?

Reflect on the spirituality and morality of your congregation. What is the quality of your congregation's spiritual life? How would you evaluate in relation to God's love for all creation your congregation's relationship with the powerless and vulnerable? Where might your congregation need to make changes in your to be more faithful in its witness to God's realm?

Continue by prayerfully examining our nation's overall spirituality and moral integrity. How does our nation reflect God's love for all creation in its relationship with the powerless and vulnerable? How would evaluate our nation's justice system? Prayerfully ask, how our judicial system be transformed to respond to God's vision of Shalom?

Make a commitment to be more mindful of the poor and powerless and to amend any spiritual and ethical shortcomings. Ask for God's blessing for you and your congregation as you seek to be more faithful to God's vision "on earth as it is in heaven.

QUESTIONS FOR REFLECTION.

1) How do you understand the scope of spirituality? How do you respond to the idea that faith is a purely personal and individual matter, my relationship with God, and has no social implications? How do you respond to the Letter of James' denunciation of faith without works of justice and hospitality?

2) In considering the future, do you think the future is decided in advance? Do you think God knows or has decided the future in its entirety? Why is this a helpful idea? Why is this a problematic idea?

3) What do you think of the idea that God changes God's mind to adapt to new situations? Can God be faithful and changing?

4) What do you think of a God for whom new things happen and who must adapt to changes in our personal life or history?

5) Do you have hope for the future? What is the source of your hope?

6) How does your congregation – or you – respond to social and political issues? In a pluralistic society, should religious institutions be involved in politics? If so, what should be their approach to political advocacy?

7) Has your faith ever inspired you to make significant personal and political/social ethical changes or sacrifices for the greater good or to be aligned with your understanding of God's vision? Have you ever been part of a protest or political advocacy as a result of your faith?

8) Is there room for persons of faith to differ on political and social issues? How do you respond to people of faith whose positions are radically different than yours? Is it appropriate to challenge fellow Christians on their political views? How can we live together with different political viewpoints? How can we practice civility toward those whose viewpoints are motivated by hatred and violence?

9) What does it mean in the USA or North America, or Europe, to "let justice roll down like waters and righteousness like an ever-flowing stream?

Prayer. God of the galaxies, seasons, and every child, I confess my complicity in economic, racial, and judicial injustice. I have not heard the cries of the poor and I turned away from the hungry and powerless. Transform me from apathy to empathy, and passivity to advocacy. Let me see you in the least of these that I might be your companion in Shalom-building, so that justice rolls down like water and righteousness like an ever-flowing streams. Amen.

CHAPTER EIGHT

A FAMINE OF HEARING GOD'S WORD

(Amos 7:1-9:10)

I will send a famine on the land;
not a famine of bread, or a thirst for water;
but of hearing the words of the Lord. (8:11)

The third section of Amos is described by scholars as the Book of Visions. After the Books of Doom and Woe, we are looking for an emotional respite. But we won't find lasting comfort in the Book of Visions. There is a brief glimmer of hope for both God and the prophet. There is the divine "perhaps" like the Ninevites' hope in Jonah. Unlike Nineveh, however, the rich and famous of the Northern Kingdom fail to repent but continue their fleecing of the poor and vulnerable. Profits once again trump the threats of God's prophets. The comfortable reassurance, born of the complacent belief, "We're God's people," "God will forgive us. It can't happen here," drowns out God's call to social transformation. Moreover, the priesthood and sanctuary are the most vocal cheerleaders for God and country and "peace, peace, when there is no peace." As Amos 7:10-17 portrays, institutional religion can be the prime agent in justifying the status quo. Institutional religion can both support and benefit from economic injustice. Endowments and contributions ease the conscience of priest and layperson alike. Institutional religion can also be mobilized to transform the social and economic order.

Amos 7:1-9:6 portrays five visions of the Northern Kingdom's future. The first two visions, these visions are not predictive but represent likely outcomes if the people don't change their ways quickly. We aren't given the mechanics of Amos' visionary experiences. It seems as if the doors of perception have been opened wide for the prophet and he is given access to God's visualization of several possible, if not likely, futures. Mystical in nature, Amos' visions give him a glimpse into the innermost experience of God, including God's emotional life, God's pathos, in response to the injustice and chicanery perpetrated by the Northern Kingdom's wealthiest citizens. Once again, prophetic mysticism is not otherworldly or abstract but drives the prophet to protest. He even protests God's apparent vindictiveness! Prophetic mysticism is profoundly concrete and historical, opening the prophet to the world of dishonest trading, foreclosures, and debt-related slavery. It may even lead to us challenging our understanding of God!

Changing God's Mind? (7:1-7:6) The Book of Amos is filled with anger, divine and human. It also reveals the depth of Amos' and God's love for this wayward people. Amos is heartbroken by what he sees. He is devastated by the pain of the vulnerable and marginalized. He feels pity for the high and mighty who will eventually be brought low. They too are God's children, and their pain, even if justly deserved, is heart-wrenching to God and the prophet from Tekoa.

A significant theological and spiritual question involves whether our prayers make any difference to God. Our response to this question will determine the shape of our ethics and hope in history and is worth reviewing once more, not only because of its theological and ethical importance but because of its significance in interpreting the prophet Amos' message. The classical theological tradition, most dramatically seen in Augustine and John Calvin, asserts that 1) God plans and executes everything in advance, that everything that happens is chosen by God in eternity; 2) God knows everything in advance in some timeless and unchanging vision: or 3) that God predestines or plans and knows everything that will occur. Divine omnipotence, the view that God has complete power such that God's will can never be thwarted, and divine omniscience, the belief that God knows everything in advance and is never surprised by human actions, nullify any form of human freedom and agency. Further, if God predestines and previews everything in advance, prayer and protest, and repentance and transformation, are rendered superfluous to God. If humans had any input in God's governance of the universe, God would be rendered imperfect and impotent, classical theologians assert. What will be will be. Any new knowledge on God's part is seen as a challenge to divine perfection since any change in God will always be for the worse. From this perspective, our belief that prayer makes a difference or that we can act to prevent evil, confront climate change, and seek justice is an illusion. On more than one occasion I have been told by "orthodox" Christians that there is no need to worry about global climate change for only God can destroy humankind or that climate patterns have been decided already and is entirely out of our hands.

Not every theologian or believer agrees with the Augustinian-Calvinist understanding of divine knowledge and power. Following the philosopher Alfred North Whitehead, process-relational and openness or open and relational theologians present an alternative to the all-determining, unchanging God, and distant God. Process and openness theology focus on the divine relativity. In contrast to Aristotle's Unmoved Mover, untouched by the world, solely contemplating itself, process theology sees God as the Most Moved Mover, touched by everything and touching everything with love. History is a call and response in which God calls with possibilities and the energy to achieve them. Humans respond to God out of their own creativity, and then God continues the process of presenting new visions in response to human choices. God works with the world as it is, intimately and lovingly inspiring it by God's vision of truth, beauty, and goodness. Our freedom is limited by God's loving presence and power, our environment, and previous choices. Our freedom reflected in positive choices also, as many scriptures suggest, provides new opportunities for God to be present in the world.

Typically, more evangelical than process theology, open theism or open and relational theology define God's power in terms of

what theologian Thomas Oord describes as God's uncontrolling
love. Love nurtures and inspires but does not dominate or coerce.
Love listens and then responds. When the world changes, God
changes. When we open God's vision, process and open and relational theologians believe that we enable God to be more active
in the world. We embrace our calling as God's partners in healing
the earth.

For a brief moment, Amos believes that there is hope for the
nation. Perhaps, they will repent and turn toward God's way of
justice. Perhaps, they just need a little more time to recognize and
respond to God's call in the "signs of the times." As Amos sees
God's vision for a wayward nation, he is horrified at what he perceives to be the likely future of the Northern Kingdom. Whether
due to God's actions or the inexorable working out of history,
death and destruction await the nation. Filled with compassion,
Amos cries out:

> O Lord God, forgive I beg you!
> How can Jacob stand?
> He is so small. (7:2)

And God hears Amos' plea. God relents and responds, "It
shall not be." (7:3)

Again, Amos is presented with a vision for a wayward land,
and again – like Moses before him – Amos begs for divine mercy.

> O Lord God, cease I beg you!
> How can Jacob stand?
> He is so small. (7:5)

God once again "relented" responding with the words "This
shall not be." (7:6) While we cannot discern God's deepest intentions for the Northern Kingdom or for America, it is clear to Amos
that God responds to human supplications. Perhaps, the compassionate as well as just God slows down the cause and effect processes
of history, the reaping and sowing process of injustice and national
collapse, to give the nation one more chance to avoid disaster.

Like a loving parent, God does not want to destroy Israel. God wants them to act in ways that will create a new future for them. God's love is strong and passionate, and sometimes threatening, but it is ultimately uncontrolling and merciful. Even the sovereign God of Amos cannot entirely control what God's people do. They must choose to follow or disregard God's vision of Shalom. Yet, within the universe, there is an arc of justice that is relentless. And, perhaps, as process and open and relational theologians aver, when we turn away from God, we diminish God's ability to inspire and energize us as persons and communities. In contrast, when we turn toward God's way, surprising possibilities emerge.

An author's typographical errors are revelatory. In the last chapter, I typed "Acts of the Possible" instead of Acts of the Apostles. That is the point, human life involves "acts of the possible," which open the door for God to act in saving and transformational ways, inviting the embrace of alternative positive futures for individuals and nations.

Tragically, the Northern Kingdom's rich and powerful continue in their injustice and dishonesty, bringing on themselves the judgments of nature and its Creator. There is no need to repeat the visions described in Amos 7-9 in all their drama and destructiveness. They build on what we have already seen: injustice leads to destruction of the nation, rich and poor alike. When we are out of alignment with the moral and spiritual arcs of history, even the non-human world suffers, and in our time its suffering leads to catastrophic changes in climate that threaten the Northern Kingdom and America.

Spirituality and Not Religion. (Amos 7:10-17) When church and state, and sanctuary and monarchy, join hands, faith always loses, and often the state is put at risk, whether in the Northern Kingdom or the United States of America. The nation takes on the characteristics of divinity, requiring our allegiance whether right or wrong, and authentic spirituality is perceived as a threat. The nation becomes our god; a god that cannot save or protect. We see the dangers of joining religion and statecraft seamlessly in Iran and in the Afghan Taliban. We also see it in the United States where many Americans identify their authoritarian political policies as blessed by an authoritarian god or view a fallible politician as God's chosen instrument of national redemption.

The binary god of nationalists in all ages must play favorites and have enemies. The enemies of the binary god are viewed as heretics, traitors, and threats to the nation as well as the true faith. America First rallies at megachurches become bastions of authoritarianism and demagoguery, undergirding white privilege, misogyny, persecution of sexual minorities and persons of color, and claims of American exceptionalism. Eclipsing Jesus, politicians become savior figures, incarnating the wishes of their wrathful and monolithic god, and giving permission to their followers to embrace their worst impulses. Prophetic voices are silenced and those who challenge the marriage of state and religion are branded as traitors and infidels. Opponents then and now are to be silenced and even killed, often by those who presume themselves to be God's pious followers. Such was Amos' fate.

In the curious interlude between visions (7:10-17), Amos is confronted by Amaziah, the chief priest of the Bethel sanctuary, who accuses the prophet of sedition, of being an enemy of the state, who has threatened the life of King Jeroboam II. Although Amaziah has not yet called in the king's police force, he has informed the king of Amos' seditious rhetoric, perhaps, in anticipation that the king will soon take action to banish or eliminate the prophet.

At first glance, Amaziah is the epitome of nationalistic religion in which religious institutions become the bastion of the status quo and seek to maintain power by silencing the voices of prophets and social critics. He represents the empire in all its moral ambiguity. Institutional religion often stifles the alternative visions that are necessary to secure justice and equity. A forerunner of Tolstoy's Grand Inquisitor and the Birmingham area pastors who criticized Martin Luther King for his employment of non-violent civil disobedience to end Jim Crow policies, Amaziah wants to preserve the religious institution's favored status even if it means stifling the voice of God. Peace and order are synonymous for the Bethel priest. Amaziah champions the nation, asserts its favored status, and promotes a sense of entitlement and security among Israel's elite. The elite are the sanctuary's best clients and supporters. They endow the priesthood, fund worship services, and expand the temple precincts. In return, they expect loyalty and priestly shibboleths proclaiming that God is on their side. "God bless Israel. We are God's chosen, and God will forgive every sin," they cry out. Centuries later, these same voices proclaim God bless America, it's "God's country, let's keep it that way." Preach generosity, the priests are told, but not social transformation or economic justice. Don't challenge our business practices, way of life, or profit motive!

Amaziah wants to rid the Bethel sanctuary of Amos, first, with the velvet glove hiding the iron fist. "Go back where you came from. If you don't love Israel, leave it. Eat your bread and make your living elsewhere." No doubt, if the soft touch doesn't work, the full force of the state will be called in to eliminate the profit.

Amaziah is an institutionalist. He knows that without the support of the king and the economic elite, the temple's place of honor will be jeopardized. Perhaps, once Amaziah felt a nearness to God's vision, perhaps he tried to effect change, but as he grew older and more established, comfort, status, and institutional survival trumped his youthful idealism. Authority is what matters. Power is necessary to preserve orthodoxy and the unique political status of the religious leadership. A big pulpit and access to the levers of power are seductive and can lure us away from the divine vision of justice and equity. Prophetic voices undermine Northern Kingdom's - and dare we say, America's - way of life and must be marginalized, silenced, or discredited. Just think about the castigating of Rev. Jeremiah Wright, whose sermons echoed those of the prophet Amos. At least, Rev. Wright's damning of America was noticed, albeit maligned, by the media, while the biblical prophets are neglected in American Christianity and politics!

Amos pushes back. "I'm not a member of the prophetic guild. I don't need a salary to be faithful to God. God called me and here

I stand and can do no other but share God's vision, regardless of the cost."

After a lifetime as a congregational pastor, university chaplain, and seminary administrator, I am aware of the pitfalls of institutional loyalty and the desire to preserve institutional viability. Prizing institutional loyalty may mean compromise and putting institutional survival over justice-seeking. It may mean going along to get along when we should draw a line between good and evil or justice and injustice. As pastors, we count the cost of discipleship, and often the cost is too great for us. We don't want to jeopardize our positions or the congregation's financial well-being. We don't want to be the objects of controversy or have our patriotism questioned. We may even receive personal threats or be asked to leave our position if we are too prophetic. We wonder if we must choose between the pastoral and prophetic aspects of spiritual leadership. In so doing, our congregations and our ministries become taillights rather than headlights in the quest for justice.

Threatened by Amaziah, Amos tells the priest the harsh truth that not only has the sanctuary lost the Spirit of God; it will eventually be destroyed as a result of its choice to serve the king rather than God. In the language of Paul Tillich, the only Ultimate that delivers is the one that stands when all else has failed. To Amaziah and to church leaders today, Amos asks, "What is your ultimate concern? Where is your loyalty? In what do you hope? Is your salvation in the nation or the grace of God? Is your savior Jesus, a politician, or your political party? Does your political vision come from the Sermon on the Mount and prophets or demagogues and manipulators? Will you follow the Prince of Peace or the Prince of Prevarication? Will you depend on right or might to save the nation?"

We don't know the temple priest Amaziah's fate. Was he carried into captivity along with his family? Or did he experience God's challenge to transform his life and ministry, to let justice roll down like waters and righteousness like an ever-flowing stream? Were his senses opened to God's challenge in the cries of the poor?

The words of Chapter 8 suggest that Amaziah chose the status quo and was complicit by his relationships with the wealthy and powerful in the coming famine of hearing God's word.

Do Amos and Amaziah Need One Another? One of the more interesting exercises you can attempt in reading the bible involves considering how the "losing party" of the argument might have expressed their position. The objects of prophetic wrath are not necessarily infidels or idolaters. Sometimes they have good, albeit fallible, reasons for their positions. For example, an imaginative and frankly liberating reading of the Bible challenges us to visualize the following events:

✓ The pain of the Egyptian parents when their first-born sons died and not just the joy of the liberated Hebrew people.

✓ The anguish of the parents of Jericho when Joshua's troops sacked the city, killing men, women, and children indiscriminately, supposedly at God's command.

✓ Peter's response to Paul's accusation of weakness when he chose not to eat with Gentiles after the "orthodox" party came to Galatia. (In Galatians, Peter is never given the chance to explain his moderate position.)

✓ The reasons members of the Jerusalem church questioned Paul's apparent undermining of the Jewish law in his ministry to the Gentiles. (Their orthodoxy is seen only as an impediment to the gospel message.)

Imaginative exercises like these prevent us from binary thinking, separating the world into heroes and villains and good and evil, based on our more informed biblical positions. Perhaps, a more inclusive reading of Amos invites us to affirm that both Amos and Amaziah can learn from each other. Amaziah needs Amos' spiritual surgery to come to his senses and recognize the problems created when the sanctuary maintains the status quo. Amaziah needs to see that his institutionalism abets the injustice of the status quo.

While Amos is the hero of the story, perhaps he needs to recognize the pressures that Amaziah faces in maintaining the positive benefits of the Bethel sanctuary. The sanctuary's survival depends on financial support. Its ability to shape society for the best, or at least prevent worse evils, requires a degree of compromise with the powers that be. Could it be that Amaziah's moderate position improves the lives of the poor in the short term, even though it cannot save the nation from ultimate destruction? Perhaps Amaziah thought he was preventing greater injustices by maintaining a moderate position, balancing support of the wealthy with care for the poor. To him, the status quo may have been preferable to social chaos that would damage the rich and poor alike.

It is the vocation of prophets to be provocative and turn the heat on. The prophetic call challenges every status quo and the limitations of every institution. This is the challenge I experienced in pastoral ministry: how to maintain institutional integrity and survival and yet be faithful to God's call to creative transformation and social criticism? Institutionalists like Amaziah are easy to critique. Yet, as we critique Amaziah, we must ask ourselves where we compromise to ensure institutional well-being. We need to balance the yin and yang of order and novelty, pastoral and prophetic, consolation and protest. This is also the challenge of prophetic protest: how much change can we demand, knowing that too much change may lead to social or institutional collapse which will harm the ones that are most vulnerable?

The Profit Motive. (8:1-10; 9:1-10) As I pen these words in Fall 2021, we are still taking down Halloween decorations and doing our best not to eat the candy our grandchildren gathered on All Hallows Eve. I spent time on All Saints and All Souls days remembering the pivotal persons in my spiritual and theological journey. In the past week, I have also seen scores of Christmas commercials and treated myself to the guilty pleasure of watching a few Hallmark Christmas movies. Especially as life returns to a new "normal" following nearly two years of Covid, it seems that it's beginning to look a lot like Christmas everywhere you go! There are no glorias to the Prince of Peace, but there are hallelujahs to the perfect gift, getting the best deal for electronics and toys, and celebrating the holiday as you've never done before with rich food, strong beverages, and conspicuous consumption. Like the days following 9/11, we are being told that the best way to recover from Covid is to "go, go, go" and "buy, buy, buy." I love the holidays and am not a curmudgeon when it comes to celebrating them with culinary delights and presents. Having shucked off Puritan abstemiousness, it seems that for America "keeping Christ in Christmas" is synonymous with purchasing and profit-making.

I am sure that Amos would have choice words for the Christian merchants and consumers, caught up in the North American Christmas frenzy. "Sixty days of shopping and one day for Jesus!" the prophet would scold. "At least give the Messiah the twelve liturgical days he deserves!"

Amos' anger is kindled at profit-making that disregards our spiritual lives and makes religion just another product to be sold. Listen to his words for the free market capitalists of the Northern Kingdom, whose fortune is made without regard to the common good or the suffering of the poorest citizens:

> Hear this, you that trample on the needy, and bring to ruin the poor of the land, saying, "When will the new moon be over so that we may sell grain; and the sabbath, so that we may offer wheat for sale? We will make the ephah small and the shekel great, and practice deceit with false balances, buying the poor for silver and the needy for a pair of sandals, and selling the sweepings of the wheat." (7:4-6)

While I don't support a return to the days of "blue laws" prohibiting commerce and festivity on Sundays and holidays, the commercialization of Christmas, Easter, and every other religious feast puts at risk not only the meaning of the incarnation and resurrection but also threatens our personal health, grounded in the need for the right balance of rest and activity, and contemplation and action. In the United States, churches and other religious communities must vie with Sunday morning youth sports and professional sporting events. Most pastors lament that sports and recreation activities usually win out over church involvement, especially in mainline and progressive congregations!

According to Amos' observations, the merchants of Samaria – and no doubt Jerusalem – are already calculating their profits as they sit down to eat their holiday dinners and celebrate the Sabbath. They have blurred the distinction between celebration and consumerism and can't wait to get back to work. Moreover, their greed means that their poorly paid employees must also get back to work, forfeiting their much-needed time for family and relaxation.

The quick profit, that's what matters, regardless of its consequences to spiritual, physical, ethical, and national wellbeing. Profit is their ultimate concern not their relationship with their families, employees, or God. Indeed, some merchants go straight from religious observances to the marketplace, getting there before the crowds to align their scales in ways that cheat their most vulnerable customers. "God is not mocked," Amos bellows. "You cannot use God to promote your self-interest. You cannot justify greed as God's will or nullify the impact of your dishonesty by donations to the temple."

Centuries later Jesus proclaimed:

> How hard it will be for those who have wealth to enter the kingdom of God!" And the disciples were perplexed at these words. But Jesus said to them again, "Children, how hard it is to enter the kingdom of God! It is easier for a camel to go through the eye of a needle than for someone who is rich to enter the kingdom of God. (Mark 10:23-25)
>
> No one can serve two masters; for a slave will either hate the one and love the other, or be devoted to the one and despise the other. You cannot serve God and wealth. (Matthew 6:24)

Harsh words from the Galilean healer! But words of the Great Physician aimed to heal our spirits, challenging values that harm our souls as well as our bodies and undermine healthy communities.

To twenty-first century North Americans, like his own 8th century BCE contemporaries, Amos exhorts, "You can't claim to love your children or grandchildren if you consume your way into planetary oblivion. Dishonesty in the marketplace and public policies that privilege the rich and powerful are an affront to God, and you and your descendants will pay the price."

Harsh words from the prophet of Tekoa! He levels the nationalistic playing field. The nations of Africa as well as Israel's neighbors, the Philistines, and the Arameans, are also loved by God. They are part of God's providence, subject both to blessing and judgment. Israel is chosen, but the universal God has a vocation – as well as judgment – for every nation. The Northern Kingdom has no special privilege. The nation will, like all nations, reap what it has sown, and suffer the consequences of their complacency and injustice.

A Famine of Hearing God's Word. (8:11-14) I believe that the heart of Amos' prophetic message can be found in two passages, one oft-quoted, the other often overlooked. Both contain a threat and an affirmation.

> Take away from me the noise of your songs; I will not listen to the melody of your harps. But let justice roll down like waters, and righteousness like an ever-flowing stream. (5:23-24)
>
> The time is surely coming, says the Lord GOD, when I will send a famine on the land; not a famine of bread, or a thirst for water, but of hearing the words of the LORD.
>
> They shall wander from sea to sea, and from north to east; they shall run to and fro, seeking the word of the LORD, but they shall not find it. (8:11-12)

A famine of hearing the words of God! Great temples, elaborate worship services carefully planned and executed, praise bands and jumbotrons, and megachurches. But sheer silence! The voice of God is muted by nationalism, consumerism, dishonest business dealings, exploitation, and privilege. God cannot be contained by our temples and churches, theologies, or doctrines, nor can God be identified with our national exceptionalism. Our religious practices will damage our spirits unless we repent our injustice and infidelity.

God is still speaking. Divine inspiration cannot be stifled by human artifice. But our ability to hear God's words is shaped by our attentiveness to God's prophets and by our repressing the sights and sounds of poverty and hopelessness.

This was a difficult message for the elite urbanites of Samaria and Jerusalem who presumed "it's just business, nothing personal" and "the Lord helps those who help themselves" as they judged the poor whose farms they were foreclosing. In the temples, the shout goes forth by the well-fed and richly attired, "God bless Israel. The apple of God's eye. We thank you for our prosperity, a sign of your blessing. We pity the poor who have drifted away from you and are suffering the consequences of their laziness. It's not our fault that they've lost their land." Yet, injustice has consequences. Apathy has consequences. Silencing prophets has consequences. God promises that there will be poverty of spirit and a famine of authentic religion if we fail to hear God's message spoken through the cries of the poor and dispossessed.

This is a difficult message for us in North America. It asserts that God has departed from the megachurches and their patriotic identification of God and country. Their god is capitalism, whiteness, and political power. They think their narrow visions of salvation can contain God, but God has left the auditorium: sound and fury, praise songs and patriotism signifying nothing, are all that remain. Yet, has our apathy, the apathy of progressives who talk and don't advocate, also deadened us to Divine Empathy? In our focusing on profits – albeit honestly, of course – have we silenced the prophets? We too are guilty bystanders, complicit in injustice and racism despite our apparent woke politics and clean hands. Despite our wokeness, energy work, green politics, and spiritual affirmations, will we experience a famine of hearing the word of God?

LISTENING TO THE PROPHET AMOS

Faith without works is dead, counsels the author of the Epistle of James. Grace abounds, God loves all of us, and Grace challenges us to be graceful in our personal lives and citizenship. A personal relationship with Jesus is of little value if it does not widen the circle of our ethical consideration and prompt us to see the divine, and nurture the well-being, in the "least of these."

Spiritual Practice. It has been said that the difference between ignorance and apathy is "I don't know" and "I don't care." These attitudes often reflect a deeper hopelessness that our planet is doomed and we can do nothing to save it, or the belief that our institutional injustices and challenges will be solved while we passively remain on the sidelines. This practice focuses on listening to the media and letting what you see and hear touch you emotionally, spiritually, and ethically. Take time to listen deeply to two ubiquitous aspects of media coverage. First, listen deeply to commercials and advertisements. What values do they emphasize? What behaviors do they encourage? What do they suggest is important? Are they helpful to your personal well-being and the well-being of the planet?

Second, listen deeply to the news, if only just the headlines. What do the stories reveal about our values, personally and institutionally? What do they suggest is important to people like us? What "signs of the times" do they portray? Prayerfully, consider where God is leading you in response to the news and advertisements. What changes in your life, or political involvement, emerge as a result of joining prayer and reflection with the media?

QUESTIONS FOR REFLECTION

1) Do you think contemporary people can have visions like Amos? Have you ever experienced a waking vision? How did you respond to that vision?

2) How do you understand divine power? Does God unilaterally decide everything that occurs? Conversely, how do you understand human – and creaturely – freedom in relationship to God? Can we choose against God? Are natural disasters and illnesses God's will?

3) How do you understand the scope of divine knowledge? Does God foresee everything in advance? If God knows everything in advance, what is the impact on human freedom and the practice of prayer?

4) Can God experience new things? What do you think of the idea of God learning new things in relationship to the world?

5) In what ways can religious institutions be sources of inspiration? Where have religious institutions been leaders in social and cultural change?

6) Listen to a sermon by Rev. Jeremiah Wright, preached during his pastorate at Trinity United Church of Christ in Chicago, Illinois. (Many are posted online.) How does Wright address the American situation? What do you think of his harsh words? How would you compare them to Amos' words to the Northern Kingdom?

7) In what ways can religious institutions be bastions of the unjust status quo? Where do you see religious institutions as a counterforce to the quest for justice?

8) What does it mean to experience a "famine of hearing God's word?" Do you think America is in danger of a famine of spiritual insight? What helps us experience God's presence in our lives and institutions? What stands in the way of experiencing God's presence in our lives and institutions?

9) Many people believe that we are in a crucial period of earth's history not only with climate change but the growing gap between the rich and poor. They are clear signs that we are

in danger. Are we attentive to signs of danger? What keeps us from responding to the signs of the times? What helps us respond to the signs of the times in life-supporting ways?

Prayer. Loving God, your word is a lamp unto my feet and a guidepost for my path. Help me remain open to your Living Word. Let me feast on your word and let me hear your voice in the cries of the poor so that I might be open to your message and inspiration, and guidance, in my life. Amen.

Chapter Nine

A Ray of Hope?

(Amos 9:11-15)

I will restore the fortunes
of my people Israel. (9:14)

I n the wake of the 2021 United Nations Climate Change
Conference (COP26), many critics claimed that while the
conference continued to make progress, it was too little, too
late. Echoing the anger of Amos, eighteen-year-old environmental
prophet Greta Thunberg, in Amos fashion, described the results
as "blah, blah, blah," that is, a torrent of words not backed up by
actions to ensure planetary wellbeing for the next generations of
humankind. Apocalyptic climate scenarios abound, many of which
are likely if we don't change our ways: the loss of coastal cities and
island nations, millions of climate-related deaths, tens of millions
of climate refugees, wars over water, hurricane and forest fire, and
governmental collapse. We seem to be "on the eve of destruction,"
as 1960's folk musician Barry McGuire warned. We must ask ourselves words as did one of my theological mentors John Cobb the
title of his pioneering work in ecological theology, *Is It Too Late?*

Amos asks, "Is it too late?" to save the nation. Is there any
hope for Israel, Judah, or frankly humankind given our proclivity
to economic injustice and self-interest? After reading eight chapters
of Amos' words of threat, woe, and doom, and the poetry of divine
violence in Amos 9;1-10, we are left with little reason to hope for
humankind to change its ways. I am sure that those who did *not*
dismiss Amos' words as alarmist and fearmongering also wondered
if there was any hope for the nation.

Scholars debate the authorship and date of the final five verses of Amos. Some believe it comes from one of Amos' proteges, perhaps two centuries later after the return of the Babylonian exiles to Judah, the Southern Kingdom. The Northern Kingdom has fallen never to rise again as a political community. But the South dreams of the possibility of new life, self-determination, and a return to the days of David.

With Amos 9:11, the tone abruptly changes. After spiritual, climatological, political, and economic catastrophe, there emerges a flicker of hope. The passionate God who has pronounced disaster on a wayward people now presents a vision of peace and prosperity. The prophet maintains that humans by their own efforts can't deliver this promise. It can only come from the hand of God.

> On that day I will raise up the booth of David that is fallen, and repair its breaches, and raise up its ruins, and rebuild it as in the days of old... I will restore the fortunes of my people Israel, and they shall rebuild the ruined cities and inhabit them; they shall plant vineyards and drink their wine, and they shall make gardens and eat their fruit. I will plant them upon their land, and they shall never again be plucked up out of the land that I have given them, says the LORD your God. (9:11, 14-15)

After catastrophe, God is going to build back better! God will repair, raise up, rebuild, restore, and plant. God will protect and nurture. God is once more "the Lord your God." While these words are addressed to a remnant of the Northern Kingdom, or hopeful members of the Southern Kingdom, they have global implications. The Ethiopians and Philistines will experience God's glory. There will be a highway through the desert, as Isaiah promises, and the desert will blossom. Verdant gardens and lush vineyards will burst forth where there was once desolation. There will be enough food and shelter for everyone. Peace will come and, again in the spirit of Isaiah's hopeful affirmation, swords will be beaten into agricultural implements, and they will learn war no more. We have a role, and it is important, though unstated, one – to be the stewards of God's new creation. To harvest the bounty of divine restoration so that all might be satisfied.

Amos' final oracle, regardless of the date of its composition, was likely treated as fantasy by many of its first listeners. After Amos' dystopian diatribe, is utopia possible, even if it is solely the result of divine intervention? After the catastrophic impact of divine judgment, is there any hope that God will renew the earth and its peoples? Restoration is simply too good to be true!

Yet, without visions of hope, we are doomed. We need a far horizon. We need to glimpse a moral and spiritual arc in the historical process to awaken to the better angels of our nature, as Abraham Lincoln hoped in an apocalyptic time of American history. We need hope to persist in confronting injustice at home and terror abroad, whether in Ukraine, Ethiopia, Central America, or in USA state legislatures and the Supreme Court. Amos asserted that this hope – and its embodiment in history – must be a work of God. God will make the changes. God will midwife the future. God will restore the nation. Although we may live in hope of a better future, we are skeptical of a divine intervention that will radically change history. The apocalyptic visions that abound in our time, the constant redating of the Second Coming of Jesus, are more hellish than heavenly. And yet we still hope for a new earth to reflect God's heavenly realm of Shalom.

The hope of a positive future for most of us today must be grounded in the impossible dream of human transformation acted out in our personal lives and political decisions. It must involve human agency as well as divine inspiration. We are God's partners in healing the world. Yet God needs us to do our part and, frankly, take the lead in incarnating God's realm of Shalom "on earth as it is in heaven." We must take seriously the words of Teresa of Avila, a strong believer in divine destiny and yet an equally strong proponent of human responsibility. I repeat them to emphasize authentic hope requires commitment and action of humankind, but not humankind in general; hope requires our willingness to claim our vocation as companions in God's vision of Shalom, however small our efforts may seem in the scheme of things.

> Yours are the hands, with which He blesses all the world.
> Yours are the hands, yours are the feet,
> Yours are the eyes, you are His body.
> Christ has no body now but yours,
> No hands, no feet on earth but yours,
> Yours are the eyes with which he looks compassion on this world.
> Christ has no body now on earth but yours.

Amos and his prophetic companions believed that God is the engine of history. History reflects God's will and power. Yet, while God has the beginnings and endings in God's care, Amos considers the possibility that we have a role to play. We can set right the scales of justice. We can forgive the debts and annul the foreclosures. We can deal fairly in the marketplace. We can look beyond self-interest to the well-being of the least of these. We can share our bounty with the dispossessed and see every person as God's beloved child, worthy of respect, affirmation, and quality of life. We can be God's hands, feet, and heart. If we are to survive as a nation and as a planet, we must expect great things of God, as Amos does, and we must, despite our fallibility and failures of the past, expect great things of ourselves.

LISTENING TO THE PROPHET AMOS

We are God's hands and feet, God's heart and mind, God's companions and innovators in responding to our current economic, racial, and ecological challenges. We have a role to play in healing the world, and we need to claim it. We need realistic hope that inspires constructive and compassionate action.

Spiritual Practice. In this final spiritual practice, take time to breathe deeply, inhaling the Breath of God. Open to divine inspiration. Feel your connection with God and all creation. After this time of centered relatedness, ponder the question: What provokes hopelessness? Visualize what threatens your sense of hope.

Then reflect on what gives you hope. What images of hope inspire you in the quest for justice and earth care? What images of hope give you strength for the journey? Visualize these images of hope and their power to change the world. Ask God to help you to hold onto hope as you seek to be God's companion in healing the world.

Questions for Reflection.

1) As you look toward the future, what threatens your hopes for the future of the nation and planet?

2) As you look toward the future, what inspires your hopes for the future of the nation and the planet?

3) What actions or relationships support your and others' hope? Where does God fit in?

4) What can your congregation do to inspire hope and agency to heal the world?

Prayer. God of all hopefulness, give me images of hope that inspire and empower. Let my life be an inspiration for others to hope. Let me claim my vocation as your companion in healing the world. Amen.

CHAPTER TEN

WHAT WOULD
AMOS SAY
TO AMERICA?

I n the course of teaching the seminar from which this book
emerged, I read not only academic studies on the Book of
Amos, many of which are listed in the bibliography but also
texts reflecting on the current American economic ethos and the
impact of our nation's history on the significant challenges we face
today.[34]   While these texts, cited below, represent diverse experiences and viewpoints and different foci, together they provide
a significant window on the American experience of wealth and
poverty in America and invite Americans to both confession and
transformation. Amos would have read these texts eagerly, noting
his own places of agreement and challenge, but also recognizing
that honest reflection on the relationship of poverty, injustice,
greed, racism, and violence is essential for healing the spirit of a

---

34 I learned from texts such as Liz Theoharis, *We Cry Justice: Reading the
Bible with the Poor People's Campaign;* Randall Balmer, *Bad Faith: Race
and the Rise of the Religious Right;* Mark Charles and Soong-Chan Rah,
*Unsettling Truths: The Ongoing, Dehumanizing Legacy of the Doctrine of
Discovery;* Nicole Hannah-Jones, *The 1619 Project: A New Origin Story;*
Obery Hendricks, *Christians Against Christianity: How Right-Wing
Evangelicals are Destroying Our Nation and Our Faith;* Stephanie Land,
Maid: Hard Work, Low Pay, and a Mother's Will to Survive; Evan Osnos,
Wildland: The Making of America's Fury; J.D. Vance, *Hillbilly Legacy: A
Memory of a Family and Culture in Crisis;* Abram Van Engen, *A City on a
Hill: A History of American Exceptionalism;* and Philip Yancey's *Where the
Light Fell.*

nation. Denial of history, whether this denial involves slavery, economic injustice, substance use disorder, the genocide of indigenous peoples, not to mention the Holocaust and climate change, dooms a nation to spiritual poverty and political dishonesty. We cannot heal what we do not face.

America is a light on a hill, but we have often put our light under a bushel basket, focusing on political power, self-interest, wealth, privilege, and superiority rather than liberty and justice for all. We are a great and mighty nation, and God sheds God's grace on us, but God's love – and judgment – is global, and our greatness is fragile, as the domestic terrorism of January 6, 2021, revealed. Our military might and economic power often hide the scars of violence and injustice, and many Americans wish to suppress any mention of slavery, Jim Crow, and the genocide of the First American settlers.

Surely Amos would have a theological and ethical field day if he were to read a recent commentary in the New York *Times*, noting that Bill Gates' birthday celebration was on a rented yacht, anchored in the Mediterranean Sea. Among the guests was Jeff Bezos, who left the party to relax on his own yacht, anticipating the completion of a new and improved $500 million yacht. Sadly, Elon Musk couldn't make it. He was at work in the United States seeking to expand his empire into the heavens!

Set those pictures of opulence next to the experiences of Stephanie Land, living in transitional housing, caring for her daughter, navigating the welfare system, and working for $10 an hour cleaning other peoples' filth, or J.D. Vance's portrait of poverty-stricken, hopeless, and opioid addicted Appalachian mother, and her traumatized children. Six months later, we were confronted by mass destruction and refugees fleeing for their lives as Russia entered a war of opportunity to occupy Ukraine, whose dictatorial overreach is mirrored by our own nation's would-be opponents of democracy. Poverty and injustice, hopelessness and fear, violence and trauma, dog persons of color as well as European Americans. The class struggle cuts across all races and the poor are begrudged any modest luxuries by middle-class Americans not to mention the children of millionaires. As Stephanie Land notes, it's hard work to be poor, not only bone grinding and soul-stifling labor, but paperwork and the ongoing justification of the need for childcare or food assistance.

I am a person of privilege living in a lovely neighborhood, with sufficient financial assets, and ample pension to travel, eat out, buy books on a whim, and give generously to our church and other socially responsible groups. I have the educational and financial privilege to be able to spend months devoted to the study, teaching, and writing that eventuated in this text. I enjoy working but no longer *have* to work as a result of retirement plans and investments. I have also briefly tasted poverty. When I was ten, my father lost his job as pastor of a small town Baptist church. With the loss of the job not only came the loss of income and social standing but a loss of a home as we needed to move from the parsonage. We settled in San Jose, California, with my professional father unemployed for several months, exhausting our family's savings and borrowing from my aunt and uncle, who regularly let us know about their generosity! We received, for a brief time, food baskets to help fill our pantry. I couldn't at the time intellectually understand what was happening. But my body did. I came down with an undiagnosed illness, feverish, congested, hallucinating, that lasted two weeks. Perhaps I was carrying the hopelessness that dominated our family's psyche. This same body-mind-spirit hopelessness is recapitulated in the experiences of millions of children, at home and abroad – Central American and Ukrainian refugees and American children caught in the multi-generational cycle of poverty.

My father finally found a job as a security guard at a semi-conductor firm and eventually returned to institutional ministry. My mother went back to school, got her teaching credential, and returned to elementary school teaching. We bought a home and were restored to the American middle class. This snapshot from my tenth year has indelibly stamped my life. Years later, my mother revealed that my father considered suicide during this time of family crisis.

For many years, regardless of having a good job and financial security, I could only view finances through the lens of scarcity. "Someday, I'll lose my job, we'll go broke, and my family will be out on the street" was a myth that was always a few inches beneath the surface. As I have grown older, these feelings of scarcity have changed. Though I am financially careful, I now look at *my* world through the lens of abundance and generosity, and the willingness not only to pay taxes for other peoples' children and social programs but a sense that helping others financially adds to my own spiritual bounty.

Like Amos, the prosperous shepherd and farmer, I feel challenged to speak on behalf of the vulnerable, to advocate for persons who can't advocate for themselves, whose voices are drowned out by the cacophony of unrestrained capitalism. I feel compelled to speak for the children, who are the most vulnerable victims of economic injustice, neighborhood violence, ecological catastrophe, and the machinations of tyrants and warmongers. I suspect Amos saw the connection between his wealth and others' poverty and that honesty and sensitivity of spirit opened him to divine inspiration. Amos heard the cries of the poor and discovered that God heard them, too, and wanted him to do something about it. And so, Amos traveled northward, struggling to be hopeful, yet preaching a message of condemnation and doom to a nation whose leaders lived in denial, not wanting to know or care about the pain of others.

Like Amos, I often feel hopeless that our nation – or the nations of the world - can change its ways, listen to the prophets, and sacrifice profits to make the changes needed for justice to roll down like water and righteousness like an ever-flowing stream and for the earth to be a place of joyful abundance and not desolation. The continuing post-election adulation of Donald Trump and the rise of Q-anon conspiracy theories and white supremacy, voter suppression, and anti-science propaganda, much of which is perpetuated in white conservative Christian churches, reveal that many would rather risk environmental and economic collapse, and destroy democracy itself, to maintain their hold on power or at least stay ahead of persons of color!

In light of the crises of our time, not significantly dissimilar to the crises Amos identified, in a pre-technological, agrarian age, I have pondered what Amos might say to us in the United States. Not attempting to channel Amos or speak for God, and fully aware of my moral and spiritual limitations and complicity in the evils I deplore, I asked for wisdom to share my version of Amos' words today, not unlike Martin Luther King's "Paul's Letter to American Christians," preached at Dexter Avenue Baptist Church, Montgomery, Alabama, November 4, 1956. King begins, perhaps with insight and oratory that inspires me to speak out as well:

> I would like to share with you an imaginary letter from the pen of the Apostle Paul. The postmark reveals that it comes from the city of Ephesus. After opening the letter I discovered that it was written in Greek rather than English. At the top of the first page was this request: "Please read to your congregation as soon as possible, and then pass it on to the other churches."

America may see itself as a light on a hill, but God's light shines on all nations. God's circle of love embraces friend and foe. God's arc of history, leaning toward Shalom, judges America and every nation as well. Let us listen to an imaginary letter of "Amos" speaking to America, praying that we might respond to God's call for our nation and the planet before it is too late.

These words are shared humbly, although I felt Amos' spirit as I typed these, praying that I might share Amos' hope for transformation of a wayward nation. And so, I pray:

> Let the words of my mouth and the meditation of my heart be acceptable to you, O LORD, my rock and my redeemer. (Psalm 19:14

+++

And the voice whispered, barely audible, as I walked in predawn Bethesda, and in the morning silence, I heard:

Listen to the words of Amos, a prophet of old, speaking to you and to your nation.

Spoken in 2022, with bombs dropping, children crying, and mothers and fathers weeping.

"A light on a hill" you claim to be and yet 140 million spirits are dimmed, struggling to stay above water, living from month to month, 18 million unable to purchase necessary medication, while billionaires frolic and politicians prevaricate. Millions of children and youth are in poverty, losing hope for the future while others tour the town in Lexus and Land Rovers, BMWs, and Mercedes Benz.

"The greatest nation in the world" and yet riddled by racism, guilty of genocide, living for the moment, consuming with abandon, with hell to pay tomorrow. Gather rosebuds while you may and leave the cleanup to future generations. Denying history and scorning science.

"Wake up from your apathy," the house is on fire. California blazes. Paradise paved once for a parking lot is now consumed by flame.

"Wake up from your complacency," waters surge, oceans rise, cities drown, and islands disappear. The baptism of death is all around us.

The earth cries "justice," the seas cry "help us," the children cry "save us."

And yet you are silent, dithering in Congress, living in denial while redwoods burn and children starve. Your denial is a death wish for your grandchildren. Chiding "welfare mothers" while encouraging billionaires to line their pockets. Arguing about child food support while corporations evade taxes.

"I am a theologian and contemplative, and not a prophet. I am a pastor, not an activist. I am a grandparent and not a protester. I am one of the favored ones, the worried well, and anxious affluent, not competent to tell others how to live their

lives, complicit in the evils I deplore, tempted to do nothing to confront the injustice that troubles me except talk, profiting while others perish."

And the voice whispered, "Pray and protest. Contemplate and agitate. Do what is in you with words and images. The world is saved one person, one moment at a time, one word and a time. Use your words for truth and beauty, justice and gentleness, and comfort and challenge. You are God's hands, feet, heart, and voice. That will be enough for now. Perhaps tomorrow you will receive a new task, a new adventure, a new calling."

Earth in the balance, nation tipped toward chaos, democracy at risk, history denied, and patriotism perverted.

"A Christian nation." And yet Caesar is supplanting Christ. I see your nation's sins, masked as virtues. God eclipsed by country. Nation first and to hell with the planet. Your savior on the golf course with Jesus entombed. The signs of the times are there – JFK Jr. will not rise again despite prayerful petitions of QAnon, but the oceans will. Hate is ignited, and love forgotten.

You say, "love your neighbor as yourself" And yet even in your churches, kindness is the victim of scorched earth rhetoric and dishonest diatribe. Falsehood won't save you, lies cannot heal you, hate can't redeem you. Church will poison you. God is God and country is not!

There is no peace. The fault is not in the stars, it is in ourselves. And a dim future waits for those awaiting the Second Coming. There will be no Second Coming as you imagine it, with us saved and the rest damned, but there may be catastrophe... the nation imperiled...the union dissolved...the better angels sent packing...the prophets persecuted to make way for profits.

And yet, perhaps they will turn. Perhaps they will see the signs of the times, writ large in fire and storm, and insurrection and incivility. Perhaps they will listen and speak for a new world, a new nation, a new spirit. Perhaps the true silent majority, the honest majority, the voice of reconciliation and compassion, the spirit of the common good, the better angels deep down in everyone will burst forth in song, protest, and celebration of a new way, so as a poet dreamed "Let America be America again."

The light grows dim. The empire crumbles. Competitors supplant. Prayer days posture and prevaricate. Traitors to truth tweet. Memes dictate theology and ethics. Hope lost. Let us eat, drink, and be merry, as we drill, baby, drill. Hopelessness masquerading as bravado.

Hoping against hope, the death of a nation can be averted. "A city on a hill" can shine with children laughing, kindness ringing, earth rejoicing, planet healing, food abounding, and diversity delivering hope. Hope for US, USA, and all creation.

I pray, dear Creator and Wise Companion, for you call us to a future with hope. I pray for us to listen. The vision of a "fallen nation" is not predetermined. It is not too late for the horizon of history can bend toward justice. "America, I cannot do it alone." says your Parent and Loved One. "You must mobilize the hands and feet of your future as you mobilize yourself for. Denouncing exceptionalism, become the exceptional people that discover the excellence in all people. The patriotic people sacrificing nation-first for planetary healing. A light on the hill shining with other lights on other hills."

The God of Every Galaxy and Each Child proclaims, "I will be with you in the valley of the shadow as you pilgrim in the twilight guided by confession and repentance as companions. I feel the pain of the vulnerable and overlooked, the single parent, the forgotten family, the hungry child, the empty-spirited bloviating billionaire."

The God of the Future promises, "I will call you to do what you deem 'impossible' – sacrifice, confession, forgiveness, and hope. I will call you to heal the spirit of the nation. I will companion you in challenge. I will guide you with my moral arc...the arc of my spirit...inclined toward justice and beauty and peace."

You must carry the burden. You must let go of the dross. Living simply and honestly, generous beyond fault, sharing greatly, sacrificing mightily. Celebrating beauty and love, song and *symphony, growth and adventure everywhere "A light for the nations" Sacrificing for the greater good. Lighting the candles of hope to illumine the pathway to healing. Glory Hallelujah!*

SELECTED
BIBLIOGRAPHY

Francis Anderson and David Noel Freedman, *Amos.* New York: Doubleday, 1989.

Bruce Birch, *Hosea, Joel, and Amos.* Philadelphia, Westminster/ John Knox, 1997.

Bruce Birch, Walter Brueggemann, Terence Fretheim, David Petersen, *A Theological Introduction to the Old Testament.* Nashville: Abingdon, 2011.

Walter Brueggemann, *The Prophetic Imagination.* Minneapolis: Fortress Press, 2001.

Goran Eidevall, *Amos.* New Haven: Yale University Press, 2017.

Bruce Epperly, *Process Theology and Politics.* Gonzales, FL: Energion, 2020.

Bruce Epperly, *Prophetic Healing: Howard Thurman's Vision of Contemplative Activism.* Friends United Press, 2020.

Abraham Joshua Heschel, *The Prophets.* Peabody, MA: Hendrickson, 1962.

Bernhard Lang, *Monotheism and the Prophetic Minority.* Sheffield, England: The Almond Press, 1983.

Howard Thurman, *Mysticism and Social Action: Lawrence Lectures and Discussions with Dr. Howard Thurman.* London: International Association for Religious Freedom, 2014. (Kindle Book)

Hans Walter Wolff, *Amos the Prophet: The Man and His Background.* Minneapolis: Fortress Press, 1973.

Hans Walter Wolff, *Joel and Amos.* Minneapolis: Fortress Press, 1977.

Gerhard von Rad, *Old Testament Theology: Israel's Prophetic Traditions.* Louisville: Westminister/John Knox, 2001.

www.ingramcontent.com/pod-product-compliance
Lightning Source LLC
Chambersburg PA
CBHW020906100426
42737CB00044B/494